COOK LITE & EAT RIGHT

The Be-Good-To-Yourself Cookbook

Favorite Recipes® of Home Economics Teachers

©Favorite Recipes Press, A Division of Great American Opportunities Inc. MCMLXXXIII
P. O. Box 77, Nashville, Tennessee 37202
Library of Congress Cataloging in Publication Data on page 128.

dear homemaker:

Home Economics — now more than ever — is vital to the quality of life because never before has the proper management of personal and public resources been so important.

Who do we find on the forefront meeting these modern challenges? The new Home Economics teacher, of course ... more professional than ever before, because today's Home Economics demands it!

In home management, it's the Home Economics teacher who's teaching young people about the dilemmas and complications of the modern home: how to manage a career and home, to keep a family healthy and happy, to develop a realistic budget in a tough economy and to stay on top of all that is new for the home and family.

As a vocational leader, today's Home Economics teacher is serving business and industry by preparing our young people for the highest quality of service in tomorrow's job market.

There is no question about it, today's amazing Home Economics teacher is a practical professional who's dedicated to making our lives easier, better, more enjoyable!

This new and exciting Be-Good-To-Yourself cookbook, *Cook Lite & Eat Right,* reflects the practical thinking of today's professional Home Economics teacher. It's a cookbook that says, "Out with heavy fats! Goodbye to too much sodium!" You'll love the results — a terrific collection of familiar and family-pleasing recipes that prove "Cooking Lite" is the best cooking of all!

There's no doubt it's the mode of the eighties, the way of the future. And it's the best way to well-rounded and delicious meals for healthy, active families.

Sincerely,

Mary Jane Blount

Mary Jane Blount
FAVORITE RECIPES PRESS

BOARD OF ADVISORS

Favorite Recipes Press wants to recognize the following who graciously serve on our Home Economics Teachers' Advisory Board:

PHYLLIS BARTON
Past President, National Association of Vocational
    Home Economics Teachers, Virginia

CHARLOTTE BOYETTE
President, New York State HET Association
Fairport, New York

PAULA HARTSFIELD
Supervisor and State FHA/HERO Advisor
Missouri Department of Elementary and
    Secondary Education

LOUANN HEINRICHS
Home Economics Teacher
Greenville, Ohio

FRANCES KING
Supervisor, Home Economics Education
Georgia Department of Education

CAROLYN KRATZ
Supervisor, Home Economics Education
Pennsylvania Department of Education

ROBERTA LOOPER
Past President, National Association of Vocational
    Home Economics Teachers, Tennessee

JANE STEIN
Home Economics Teacher
San Diego, California

contents

be good to yourself

The bounty of our country is reflected on our family dining tables day after day. Picture it! Colorfully delicious fruit and vegetables. Juicy, tender cuts of beef and pork. Succulent fish and fowl varieties. A taste-tempting array of breads and cereals. And last but not least, a famous selection of memorable desserts and sweets. In addition, the American homemaker understands the practical aspect of using this bounty of food to create balanced and nutritious meals for her family.

There's more to presenting a pleasing and healthful menu than meets the eye. First, there's the calorie! Necessary and unavoidable, but still the cause of over-weight when too many are included in the menu. As a result, weight-conscious menu planners are becoming calorie counters. Then there's sodium, cholesterol and satu-rated fats. More and more Americans are learning to watch their intake of these, and their health is better off for it.

Best of all, people everywhere are "Cooking Lite and Eating Right" and enjoying it!

why reduce sodium intake?

Like other nutrients in a balanced diet, sodium (salt) is beneficial and necessary in proper amounts. Doctors prescribe a sodium-restricted diet for persons who suffer from various ailments. Studies point out that everyone can benefit from scrutinizing their sodium intake. Because processed foods are so common to our modern menu, sodium preservatives are pervasive in our diets. We take in far more sodium than our body really needs. And as studies indicate, it may be this overconsumption of salts in our diet that leads to some of the health problems requiring a medically pre-scribed low-sodium diet.

Luckily, it is relatively simple to cut down on unnecessary salt in your menus. First of all, become a label reader. Be on the lookout for additives such as sodium benzoate, sodium sulphite, sodium bicarbonate, baking soda and a long list of other preservatives used in food processing. Packaged luncheon meats, cured ham, hot dogs, bacon or sausage, as well as a host of condiments including mustard, pickles, relish, savory sauces for meats, and spreads for sandwiches are especially high in sodium. But compare labels and you will find that there are foods available that go easy on the sodium additives and preservatives. Additive-free processed foods are available in the natural food section of grocery stores or in your neighborhood natural and health food stores.

If the thought of reducing salt in your menu leaves you believing your meals will be dull and tasteless, take heart! Usually, the amount of table salt (sodium chloride)

most cooks use while cooking is minimal compared to the additive/preservative source of sodium in the average diet. Eliminate or reduce these and the table salt is really not a problem. If you also choose to reduce the use of table salt, there are several tasty options. "Lite" table salt is commonly available, as well as a full array of delicious herbs, spices, and other seasonings to use in cooking and at the table. The result will be exciting taste treats, variety, and interest for your menu. Remember, "Cooking Lite to Eat Right" does not mean you have to take sodium completely out of your diet. It only means that you monitor and even greatly reduce your family's sodium intake while still enjoying a delicious menu.

reducing cholesterol & saturated fats

Americans are also learning the benefits of reducing the intake of cholesterol and saturated fats in their diets. Like salt, fats are a very important part of balanced nutrition. Too much fat and the wrong kinds of fat are unhealthy.

Cholesterol is normally present in the blood stream, but becomes dangerous when present along with too many saturated fats. These two work together to thicken and even clog the arteries by building up inside the artery wall. The process generally takes years. It is when the arteries surrounding the heart and brain become thickened and clogged that disabling and fatal heart attacks or strokes often occur. Cholesterol, found in egg yolks, shellfish, duck and goose, organ meats and various other foods need not be eliminated or greatly reduced unless required by a physician. If you are concerned about your cholesterol intake, consult your doctor.

The use of saturated fats can and should be greatly reduced from the diet. This is easily accomplished by replacing foods high in saturated fats with polyunsaturated fats, low-fat and nonfat items, and lean foods. Again, become a label reader. Butter, whole milk, sour cream and cream, chocolate, coconut and palm oils, as well as hydrogenated margarines, shortenings, and peanut butter are common sources of saturated fats. Hidden sources include nondairy creamer, commercially prepared bakery goods and snacks, plus crackers and breads, cakes, and cookie mixes. All animal fats are saturated fats. So a low-fat diet should concentrate on poultry, fish, and lean cuts of meat, as well as "lite" cheeses, polyunsaturated oils and margarine, plus nonfat or low-fat milk and milk products. Home-baked goods should be prepared with polyunsaturated oil or margarine, low-fat milk, and even cholesterol-free egg substitutes. As an added bonus, a low-fat diet usually means fewer calories (except for the margarine and oils) in the diet. That's good news for everyone!

"Cook Lite & Eat Right" — means change in your cooking and eating habits. But it doesn't have to mean less enjoyment at mealtimes. In fact, lighter meals can be zestier meals, fresher and tastier. And you will know you are doing the very best for yourself and your family!

appetizers
& snacks

ANTIPASTO

1 clove of garlic, crushed
1/4 c. olive oil
1/4 c. wine vinegar
1 16-oz. can artichoke hearts, drained
1 16-oz. can green beans, drained
1 16-oz. can asparagus, drained
1 lg. cantaloupe, peeled, sliced in wedges
1/2 lb. prosciutto, sliced thin

Combine .... first 3 ingredients in shallow bowl.
Marinate .... artichoke hearts, green beans and asparagus in mixture overnight in refrigerator; drain.
Wrap .... each melon wedge in 1 slice prosciutto.
Arrange ..... with marinated vegetables on serving dish.
Garnish ..... with tomato wedges and radishes.

Mary Lou Brown
Musical, Tennessee

BACON-WRAPPED WATER CHESTNUTS

1 8-oz. can water chestnuts, drained
1/4 c. soy sauce
1 lb. bacon

Marinate .... water chestnuts in soy sauce for 1/2 hour; drain.
Cut .... bacon strips into halves.
Wrap .... each water chestnut in bacon strip.
Secure ...... with toothpick.
Place .... on rack in baking pan.
Bake .... at 400 degrees for 20 minutes.
Serve .... hot.

Kimberly Dunn
Seattle, Washington

DEVILED EGGS

6 hard-boiled eggs
1/4 c. cream-style cottage cheese
2 tbsp. skim milk
1 tbsp. snipped parsley
1 tsp. vinegar
1 tsp. prepared mustard
Salt and pepper to taste
1/4 tsp. prepared horseradish

Slice .... eggs lengthwise.
Remove .... yolks; place in blender container with remaining ingredients.
Process ..... until well blended, scraping sides occasionally.
Spoon ...... mixture into egg whites.
Garnish ..... with parsley.

Enid Craig
Ardmore, Oklahoma

THREE-CHEESE BALL

1/2 lb. sharp Cheddar cheese, softened
2 3-oz. packages cream cheese, softened
1/4 lb. blue cheese, softened
1 tsp. grated onion
1 tbsp. Worcestershire sauce
1 tsp. parsley flakes
Chopped stuffed olives to taste
1/2 c. chopped pecans

Combine .... cheeses in bowl, mixing well.
Add .... remaining ingredients, reserving 1/4 cup pecans; mix well.
Shape ...... into ball.
Roll .... in reserved pecans.
Chill .... until serving time.

Jill Harris
Flower, Massachusetts

HIGH-FIBER MEATBALLS

2 eggs, beaten
1/3 c. milk
1/3 c. bran
1 lb. lean hamburger
1 lb. coarsely chopped mixed pork and veal
1 stalk celery, minced
1 med. onion, finely chopped
2 tsp. salt
2 tbsp. Worcestershire sauce
1 tbsp. oil

Combine .... all ingredients except oil in bowl, mixing well.
Shape ...... into 1-inch balls.
Brown ...... in hot oil in skillet; drain.
Place .... in casserole.
Bake .... covered, at 350 degrees for 30 minutes.

Jo Ann Melrose
New Brighton, Minnesota

CRISPY DRUMSTICKS WITH HONEY SAUCE

3 lb. miniature drumsticks
1 c. flour
2 tsp. salt
1/4 tsp. pepper
2 tsp. paprika
1/2 c. butter
1/4 c. honey
1/4 c. lemon juice

Coat .... drumsticks in flour seasoned with salt, pepper and paprika.
Melt .... butter in shallow baking pan.
Arrange ..... drumsticks in single layer in pan, turning to coat.
Bake .... at 400 degrees for 30 minutes.
Pour .... honey in a fine stream into lemon juice in bowl, beating constantly.
Turn .... drumsticks; cover with honey mixture.
Bake .... for 10 minutes longer or until tender, basting occasionally.

Mrs. Brenda L. Little
Farmville, North Carolina

LOW-CALORIE SHRIMP APPETIZER

1/2 c. finely chopped shrimp
2 tsp. finely chopped parsley
1 tbsp. grated onion
1 hard-boiled egg, chopped
1 tbsp. low-calorie mayonnaise
12 2-in. celery sticks

Combine .... first 5 ingredients in bowl, mixing well.
Stuff .... into celery sticks.
Chill .... thoroughly.

Carolyn Rock
Benton, Wisconsin

EGGPLANT CRISPS

1 c. sliced eggplant
1 tsp. salt
1 egg, slightly beaten
1 tsp. mayonnaise
1/8 tsp. butter-flavored salt
1 slice white bread
1 oz. Cheddar cheese
1/4 tsp. dry onion flakes

Soak .... eggplant slices in 3/4 cup salted water in bowl for 20 minutes.
Drain ...... and pat dry.
Blend ...... egg, mayonnaise and butter-flavored salt in small bowl.
Place .... bread, cheese and onion flakes in blender container.
Process ..... until finely crumbled.
Dip .... eggplant slices into egg mixture, then into crumb mixture.
Place .... in baking dish.
Bake .... at 450 degrees for 15 minutes or until lightly browned and crisp, turning once.
Yields ...... 1 serving.

Fern Hill
Broomfield, Colorado

HAWAIIAN GRAB BAG

1 1/2 c. cottage cheese
1/2 c. salad dressing
1/2 c. yogurt
Grated horseradish to taste
1/2 tsp. monosodium glutamate
2 tsp. dry mustard
1/2 tsp. salt
1 tbsp. lemon juice
1 c. cherry tomatoes
1 c. cucumber wedges
1 c. marinated artichokes
1 c. green pepper chunks
1 c. sliced water chestnuts
1 c. avocado chunks
1 c. marinated mushrooms
1 c. cooked cold shrimp
1 c. cooked chicken livers

Place .... cottage cheese and salad dressing in blender container.
Process ..... until smooth.
Add .... next 6 ingredients, mixing well.
Chill .... in refrigerator overnight.
Place .... remaining vegetables, shrimp and livers in large serving bowl, mixing well.
Pour .... sauce over mixture, tossing to coat.
Serve .... with wooden picks.

Jane Nessler
Bosco City, Illinois

RIPE OLIVE RIGOLETTOS

2 8-oz. packages cream cheese, softened
1 tsp. salt
6 drops of red pepper seasoning
2 tbsp. lemon juice
2 tbsp. tomato paste
1 1/2 c. ripe olives, finely chopped
1/2 c. mashed avocado
8 candied cherries, chopped
1 tbsp. chopped ginger
1/4 c. chopped nuts
1 bunch hearts of celery
Green peppers
Tomatoes
Onions
Cucumbers, sliced
Cheddar cheese triangles

Blend ......cream cheese with next 3 ingredients in bowl.
Divide ......into 3 portions.
Mix ....tomato paste with half the olives into 1 portion; avocado and remaining olives into second portion; cherries, ginger and nuts into third portion.
Stuff ....celery stalks with cherry mixture; press into bunch.
Chill ....wrapped in waxed paper, for several hours.
Cut ....green peppers and tomatoes into wedges, removing seeds and membranes.
Cut ....onions into wedges and separate.
Pipe ....cheese mixtures onto vegetable and cheese canape bases.
Cut ....celery bunch into slices.
Garnish .....with olive slices.
Chill ....until serving time.

Photograph for this recipe on page 7.

PINK PICKLED EGGS

6 hard-boiled eggs
1 c. canned beet juice
1 c. cider vinegar
1/2 bay leaf
1/4 tsp. ground allspice
1 clove of garlic, crushed
1 tsp. salt
Pepper to taste

Place ....eggs in 1-quart jar.
Combine ....remaining ingredients in bowl, mixing well.
Pour ....over eggs.
Chill ....covered, for 8 hours.
Slice ....before serving.

Mrs. John C. Lint
Grand Junction, Iowa

RIPE OLIVE QUICHE

1 10-oz. package frozen patty shells, thawed
1 8-oz. package cream cheese, softened
2 eggs
2 c. chopped ripe olives
1 2-oz. can rolled anchovies with capers
1/2 c. grated Fontina cheese
1/2 c. grated Parmesan cheese

Knead ......patty shells together.
Roll ....on floured surface.
Press ....into 10-inch fluted tart pan.
Combine ....cream cheese with eggs in bowl, mixing well.
Pour ....into prepared tart pan.
Top ....with olives, anchovies and cheeses.
Bake ....at 400 degrees for 40 minutes or until brown.
Serve ....warm or cold.
Yields ......20 servings.

Photograph for this recipe on page 7.

 Keep oil in shaker-topped bottle. A few drops will do the job of more.

BROILED CRAB NIBBLES

1 6 1/2-oz. can crab
1/4 c. minced onion
1 c. shredded American cheese
1 c. mayonnaise
French bread slices

Combine ....first 4 ingredients in bowl, mixing well.
Spread .....on French bread slices.
Broil ....until brown and bubbly.
Serve ....hot.

Eleanor V. Harmon
Scobey, Montana

TANGY TUNA BALLS

1 7-oz. can water-pack tuna, drained
1 3-oz. package Neufchatel cheese, softened
2 tbsp. finely chopped celery
2 tsp. lemon juice
1/2 tsp. Worcestershire sauce
Salt to taste
Parsley, finely snipped

Combine .... first 6 ingredients in bowl, mixing well.
Shape ...... into small balls.
Roll .... in parsley.
Chill .... several hours.
Serve .... with cocktail picks.

Charlene Turner
Redding, Pennsylvania

FRUITY FRUIT DIP

1 8-oz. carton yogurt
3 tbsp. low-calorie orange marmalade
1/4 tsp. ground cinnamon
Green grapes
Apple wedges
Cantaloupe balls
Pineapple chunks

Combine .... first 3 ingredients in bowl, mixing well.
Chill .... to serving temperature.
Place .... in dip bowl and serve with chilled fruit.

Bonnie Dunlap
Salisbury, North Carolina

WHITE SPICE DIP FOR FRUIT SLICES

1 c. sour cream
1 tbsp. freshly ground horseradish
1 tsp. lemon juice
2 drops of Worcestershire sauce
Salt to taste
1 tsp. pepper
Apple slices

Combine .... all ingredients except apple slices in small bowl, mixing well.
Serve .... with crisp apple slices.

Photograph for this recipe on page 12.

CAPERS DIP

1 8-oz. package cream cheese, softened
Dash of garlic salt
1 3-oz. bottle of capers, drained

Combine .... all ingredients in bowl, mixing well.
Chill .... for several hours.
Serve .... with crackers.

Betty Johns
Tacoma, Washington

COTTAGE CHEESE-ONION DIP

1 pt. cottage cheese
1 pkg. dry onion soup mix
2 tbsp. lemon juice

Process ..... cottage cheese in blender container until smooth.
Add .... remaining ingredients, processing until well blended.
Serve .... with crackers or fresh vegetables.
Yields ...... 2 cups.

Mrs. Laurena Ward
Ashford, Alabama

DIETER'S CHIP DIP

1 lb. cream-style cottage cheese
1/4 c. mayonnaise
1/4 tsp. garlic salt
1/4 tsp. Worcestershire sauce

Combine .... all ingredients in blender container.
Process ..... until smooth.
Serve .... with chips or fresh vegetables.

Georgia Geiger
Livonia, Michigan

GARLIC VEGETABLE DIP

2 8-oz. cartons yogurt
1 env. cheese and garlic salad dressing mix
1 tbsp. dried chives
1/2 tsp. dried parsley flakes

Combine .... all ingredients in bowl, blending well.
Chill .... covered, for several hours.
Serve .... with fresh vegetables.
Yields ...... 2 cups.

Mrs. Glenna Hunsinger
Mineral Point, Wisconsin

CHEESY HERB DIP

1 c. low-calorie mayonnaise
1 3-oz. package Neufchatel cheese, softened
1 tsp. mixed salad herbs, crushed
Salt to taste
1 tbsp. snipped parsley
1 tbsp. grated onion
1/2 tsp. Worcestershire sauce
2 tsp. capers, drained

Combine ....all ingredients in blender container.
Process .....until smooth.
Chill ....for several hours.
Serve ....with fresh vegetables.

Margaret Mudor
Pensacola, Florida

IRMA'S SNACK DIP

1 24-oz. carton sm. curd cottage cheese, at room temperature
1 8-oz. package cream cheese, softened
1 4-oz. package blue cheese, softened
1/4 tsp. garlic salt
1/4 tsp. onion salt

Combine ....all ingredients in mixer bowl.
Beat ....with electric mixer until well blended.
Serve ....with crackers or chips.

Irma Zelenka
Omaha, Nebraska

THREE-CHEESE DUNK

1 c. cottage cheese, well drained
1 c. grated Cheddar cheese
2 oz. blue cheese, mashed
2 tbsp. mayonnaise
1 tbsp. horseradish
1 tsp. mustard
1/2 tsp. Worcestershire sauce
3 green onions, finely chopped
1/2 tsp. each salt, celery salt
Pepper to taste
Sliced apples

Blend ......cheeses in bowl.
Add ....remaining ingredients except apples, mixing well.
Serve ....with crisp apple slices.

Photograph for this recipe on this page.

REGENCY DIP

1 8-oz. carton small-curd cottage cheese
2/3 c. yogurt
1 tbsp. fresh chopped parsley
1/2 lb. mushrooms, finely chopped
1/2 c. finely diced celery
1/4 c. coarsely chopped water chestnuts
1 tbsp. minced onion
1 tbsp. lemon juice

Combine ....first 3 ingredients in blender container.
Process .....until smooth.
Stir ....in remaining ingredients.
Chill ....to serving temperature.
Serve ....with fresh vegetables.

Shirley Woods
Birmingham, Alabama

ZUCCHINI DIP

2 med. zucchini, diced, cooked
1 tbsp. chopped onion
1/2 c. tomato juice
Salt to taste
1/8 tsp. basil
1 8-oz. package Neufchatel cheese, softened
1 tbsp. bacon bits

Combine ....first 6 ingredients in blender container.
Process .....until smooth.
Chill ....overnight.
Stir ....in bacon bits just before serving.
Serve ....with Melba toast or vegetables.
Yields ......1 2/3 cups.

Willette Jerome
Santa Cruz, New Mexico

FRESH VEGETABLE PLATTER

1   8-oz. carton yogurt
1   3-oz. package cream cheese
1/2 c. mayonnaise
1 tsp. Worcestershire sauce
3 to 4 drops of hot sauce
1/4 tsp. garlic salt
1 tbsp. garlic salad dressing mix
Zucchini strips
Celery sticks
Cucumber sticks
Carrot sticks
Cauliflowerets

Combine .... first 7 ingredients in blender container.
Process ..... until well blended.
Serve .... in bowl in center of large platter surrounded by vegetables.

Kathy Tomlin
Gary, Ohio

EASY VEGGIE DIP

1/2 c. low-calorie mayonnaise
1/4 c. cottage cheese
1/2 c. grated Cheddar cheese
1 tsp. chopped onion
2 tsp. parsley flakes
1/2 tsp. lemon juice

Combine .... all ingredients in blender container.
Process ..... until well mixed.
Serve .... with fresh chilled vegetables.

Mrs. Connie Amendola
Johnsonburg, Pennsylvania

YOGURT DIP

1/4 c. mayonnaise
1/2 c. low-fat yogurt
1/2 tsp. dry mustard
1/2 tsp. curry powder
Salt and pepper to taste

Combine .... all ingredients in bowl, mixing well.
Garnish ..... with dill.
Serve .... with fresh vegetables.

Mrs. Beverly Sachs
Thornwood, New York

DELICIOUS CLAM SPREAD

1   7 1/2-oz. can minced clams
1/2 lb. cottage cheese
1/2 sm. onion, grated
1 tsp. Worcestershire sauce
Dash of garlic salt
1 tsp. celery salt

Drain ...... clams, reserving 1 tablespoon liquid.
Place .... clams and cottage cheese in blender container.
Process ..... until smooth.
Add .... reserved liquid and remaining ingredients.
Process ..... until smooth.
Chill .... to serving temperature.
Spread ..... on vegetable slices.

Sande J. Speck
Watertown, Minnesota

SCALLOPS WITH CAT-PIC DIP

1   8-oz. carton yogurt
1/4 c. catsup
2 tbsp. finely chopped sweet pickle
1/2 tsp. prepared mustard
Salt to taste
1   12-oz. package frozen scallops, cooked

Combine .... first 5 ingredients in bowl, mixing well.
Chill .... to serving temperature.
Place .... on serving tray surrounded by chilled scallops.

Jane Berry
Reading, Pennsylvania

CHEESY SHRIMP DIP

1   8-oz. carton farmer cheese
3 tbsp. skim milk
1 tsp. prepared horseradish
1   5-oz. jar Neufchatel cheese spread with pimento
Dash of Tabasco
1   12-oz. package frozen shrimp, cooked

Combine .... first 5 ingredients in bowl, beating until fluffy.
Chill .... to serving temperature.
Serve .... with shrimp.

Jean Hagan
Cheboygan, Wisconsin

BLENDER TUNA DIP

1 sm. can tuna, undrained
1 c. salad dressing
1/4 c. sliced pimento-stuffed olives
1/4 tsp. onion salt
1/4 tsp. celery salt
1/4 c. lemon juice

Combine .... all ingredients in blender container.
Process ..... until smooth.
Serve .... with vegetables, crackers or chips.
Yields ...... 1 3/4 cups.

Roberta Tuckahoe
Richmond, Virginia

Never skip meals.

CORN CHILI CHIPS

3 tbsp. oil
1/2 c. buttermilk
1/2 c. yellow cornmeal
1/2 c. toasted cornmeal
1/2 c. whole wheat pastry flour
3/4 tsp. salt
1/4 tsp. soda
1/8 tsp. cayenne pepper
1/2 tsp. chili powder
Paprika

Add .... oil to buttermilk, mixing well.
Stir .... next 7 ingredients together in bowl.
Add .... liquid, stirring until dough clings together.
Knead ...... for about 5 minutes on floured board.
Roll .... 1/2 at a time into 12-inch square.
Cut .... into 1-inch squares.
Sprinkle .... with paprika.
Place .... on lightly greased baking sheet.
Bake .... at 350 degrees for 15 minutes or until lightly browned; cool slightly.
Remove .... from baking sheet to wire rack to cool.
Store .... in covered container.
Yields ...... 8 to 10 dozen.

Samantha Egger
Brentwood, Vermont

OATMEAL-HONEY CRACKERS

3 c. whole wheat flour
2 c. oats
1/4 c. warmed honey
1 tsp. salt
1/3 tsp. soda
1/2 c. butter
3/4 c. (about) buttermilk, heated

Mix .... first 6 ingredients in bowl.
Add .... buttermilk gradually, mixing well after each addition to form cookie-type dough.
Roll .... half the dough at a time, between waxed paper to 3/16-inch thickness.
Cut .... into 1-inch squares; prick with fork.
Arrange ..... on greased baking sheet.
Bake .... at 325 degrees for 25 minutes or until lightly browned.
Store .... in airtight container.
Yields ...... 12 dozen.

Patty Cardwell
New Haven, Connecticut

POPPY SEED CRACKERS

1/3 c. poppy seed
2 c. whole wheat pastry flour
1 1/2 tsp. salt
1/2 tsp. soda
1/3 tsp. pepper
1/3 c. oil
1 tsp. honey
1 egg, slightly beaten
1/4 c. minced onion

Combine .... poppy seed with 1/3 cup boiling water; cool.
Sift .... flour, salt, soda and pepper into bowl.
Stir .... in remaining ingredients and poppy seed mixture, mixing well.
Knead ...... lightly on floured surface until smooth.
Roll .... out, 1/2 at a time, on lightly floured board to 1/8-inch thickness.
Cut .... with 1 1/2-inch biscuit cutter.
Place .... on baking sheet; prick with fork.

Bake .... at 425 degrees for 10 minutes or until lightly browned.
Store .... in airtight container.
Yields ...... 8 dozen.

Vinci Martin
Pittsburgh, Pennsylvania

 Almonds are a nutritious natural food and provide a high nutrient density compared to the calories consumed.

WHOLE WHEAT-CHEDDAR CRACKERS

1/2 lb. Cheddar cheese, grated
1 c. whole wheat flour
3 tbsp. oil
1/4 tsp. salt
Dash of cayenne pepper
1/4 c. milk
1/3 c. chopped walnuts
Walnut halves

Mix .... first 5 ingredients in bowl until crumbly.
Add .... milk and chopped walnuts, mixing well.
Shape ...... into 1-inch balls; flatten.
Top .... with walnut halves.
Arrange ..... on cookie sheet.
Bake .... at 350 degrees for 20 minutes or until lightly browned.
Yields ...... 2 1/2 dozen.

Theresa Neal
Palouse, Washington

CHILI RAISINS

1 lb. raisins
1 c. oil
Salt
Chili powder

Combine .... raisins and oil in saucepan.
Simmer ..... for 10 minutes or until raisins are plump; drain.
Sprinkle .... with salt and chili powder.
Yields ...... 10 to 12 servings.

Joan Berry
Traverse City, Maryland

CURRIED WALNUTS

2 c. walnuts
2 tbsp. oil
1 tsp. salt
1/2 tsp. (or more) curry powder
Pinch of sugar
1/4 tsp. garlic powder

Cook .... walnuts in oil in skillet until golden; drain on paper towels.
Sprinkle .... with remaining ingredients; cool.
Store .... in airtight container.
May .... substitute paprika, chili powder or pumpkin pie spice for garlic powder.

Pat Roberts
Bacon Raton, Florida

CINNAMON-COFFEE PECANS

2 tsp. instant coffee
1/4 c. sugar
1/4 tsp. cinnamon
Dash of salt
1 1/2 c. pecan halves

Combine .... all ingredients in saucepan with 2 tablespoons water.
Simmer ..... for 3 minutes, stirring constantly.
Spread ..... on waxed paper using 2 forks to separate pecans.

Vivian Pierson
Paxton, Illinois

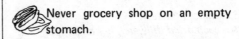 Never grocery shop on an empty stomach.

TOASTED PUMPKIN SEED

Fresh pumpkin seed
1 to 2 tbsp. melted butter
Salt, garlic salt or onion salt to taste

Rinse ...... pumpkin seed; pat dry with paper towels.
Spread ..... on shallow baking sheet.
Drizzle ..... with butter and sprinkle with salt.
Bake .... at 325 degrees for 1 1/2 hours or until brown, stirring every 10 minutes.

Mrs. Darrell Dunlap
Dysart, Iowa

SAVORY SUNFLOWER SEED

1 tsp. butter
1 tsp. oil
1 c. sunflower seed
1 tsp. chopped chives
1/2 tsp. celery salt

Heat . . . . butter and oil in small skillet.
Add . . . . sunflower seed with chives and celery salt.
Toast . . . . . . for 8 minutes, stirring occasionally; drain.
Yields . . . . . . 1 cup.

Melba Price
Tampa, Florida

DILLY CHIVED POPCORN

1 tbsp. oil
3 c. popped popcorn
1/2 tsp. chopped chives
1/2 tsp. dillweed
1 tsp. grated Parmesan cheese
1/2 tsp. celery salt

Heat . . . . oil in heavy skillet.
Add . . . . popped popcorn and seasonings.
Cook . . . . for 5 minutes, stirring occasionally.
Yields . . . . . . 3 cups.

Peg Martin
Adair, Georgia

HARVEST SNACK MIX

1/3 c. melted butter
1 tsp. each dried dillweed, lemon-pepper marinade
1 tsp. Worcestershire sauce
1/2 tsp. each onion powder, garlic powder
1/4 tsp. salt
2 qt. popped popcorn
2 c. canned shoestring potatoes
1 c. mixed nuts

Combine . . . . butter and seasonings in large bowl, mixing well.
Add . . . . remaining ingredients, tossing to mix.
Spread . . . . . on baking sheet.
Bake . . . . at 350 degrees for 6 minutes or until brown, stirring once.

Judith Brown
Rawlins, Wyoming

CARAWAY-CURRY SPREAD

2 3-oz. packages cream cheese, softened
1 tbsp. milk
1 tbsp. caraway seed
1/2 tsp. curry powder
Dash each of hot pepper sauce, salt
Sliced apples

Combine . . . . all ingredients except apples in small bowl, blending well.
Chill . . . . until serving time.
Serve . . . . with crisp apple wedges.
Yields . . . . . . 1 cup.

Photograph for this recipe on page 12.

HERB CHEESE

1 1/2 lb. sharp Cheddar cheese, shredded
2 tbsp. each minced parsley, chives
2 tbsp. each thyme, sage, savory
1/2 c. cream
2/3 c. Sherry

Combine . . . . all ingredients in bowl, mixing well.
Chill . . . . overnight.
Force . . . . . . through strainer.
Yields . . . . . . 4 cups.

Photograph for this recipe on page 12.

GOUDA PARTY SPREAD

1 8-oz. Gouda cheese, softened
1 3-oz. package smoked beef, chopped
1/4 c. sour cream
1/2 tsp. prepared mustard
1/4 tsp. Worcestershire sauce
Dash of hot sauce
1/8 tsp. garlic salt
1 tbsp. each pickle relish, minced green pepper, minced pimento

Cut . . . . thin slice from top of cheese shell.
Scoop . . . . . . out cheese, reserving shell.
Combine . . . . cheese with remaining ingredients in bowl; mixing well.
Fill . . . . reserved shell with mixture.
Serve . . . . on bed of greens with crackers or chips.

Robin Sands
White Mountain, Vermont

soups & sandwiches

soups

CHILLED GAZPACHO

1 c. finely chopped peeled tomatoes
1/2 c. each finely chopped celery,
    cucumber, green pepper, onion
2 tsp. finely chopped parsley
1/4 tsp. minced garlic
3 tbsp. wine vinegar
2 tbsp. oil
1/4 tsp. pepper
1 tsp. salt
2 to 2 1/2 c. tomato juice

Combine .... all ingredients in bowl.
Chill .... covered, for 4 hours or longer.
Serve .... cold.

Elaine Moore
Hector, Minnesota

COOL AND TANGY SOUP

2 lg. cucumbers, peeled, sliced
1/2 tsp. salt
1 1/2 tsp. sugar
1 tbsp. olive oil
1 c. yogurt

Combine .... all ingredients in bowl, mixing
    well.
Chill .... for 2 hours or longer.
Place .... in blender container.
Process ..... for 20 seconds.
Pour .... into bowls.
Garnish ..... with cucumber slices and fresh
    dill.

Francie Helpmann
Blue Hill, Nebraska

BROCCOLI CHOWDER

4 c. chopped fresh broccoli
4 chicken bouillon cubes
2 c. skim milk
8 oz. tuna, flaked
2 tsp. salt
1/4 tsp. pepper
1/2 c. evaporated skim milk
4 oz. Swiss cheese, grated
1/2 tsp. imitation butter flavoring

Combine .... first 2 ingredients with 1 cup
    water in large saucepan.
Simmer ..... for 7 minutes or until broccoli is
    tender-crisp.
Stir .... in remaining ingredients with 3
    cups water.
Heat .... to serving temperature.
Yields ...... 4 servings.

Mildred M. Fait
Sparks, Nevada

CREAM OF FRESH VEGETABLE SOUP

3 med. potatoes, finely chopped
1/3 c. sliced sm. onions
1/2 c. thinly sliced carrots
1/2 c. chopped celery
1/2 c. cut green beans
1/2 c. peas
3 c. milk
1/4 c. butter
1 3/4 tsp. salt
1/2 tsp. pepper

Combine .... potatoes with 2 cups boiling
    water in saucepan.
Simmer ..... until tender.
Mash .... potatoes in saucepan.
Add .... remaining vegetables.
Simmer ..... until tender.
Add .... milk, butter, salt and pepper.
Heat .... to serving temperature.
Yields ...... 4 to 5 servings.

Grace Luther
Camrose, South Carolina

FRECKLED POTATO SOUP

1 qt. chicken broth
2 med. potatoes, chopped
1 c. coarsely chopped watercress
Salt and pepper to taste
1 c. skim milk

Combine .... first 3 ingredients in saucepan.
Simmer ..... covered, until potatoes are
    tender.
Stir .... in remaining ingredients, mash-
    ing potatoes with spoon.
Heat .... to serving temperature.
Serve .... with wheat germ biscuits.

Andrea, O'Roarke
Dallas, Texas

TOMATO SOUP WITH CHEESY DUMPLINGS

1 c. tomato juice
1/4 tsp. Worcestershire sauce
1/2 tbsp. instant nonfat dry milk
1 lb. Cheddar cheese, grated
1 slice bread, crumbled
1 egg, slightly beaten
Salt and pepper to taste

Combine .... first 3 ingredients with 1/2 cup cheese in saucepan.
Cook .... over low heat until cheese melts, stirring constantly.
Place .... remaining ingredients in blender container with remaining cheese.
Process ..... until smooth.
Shape ...... into dumplings.
Drop .... into soup mixture.
Simmer ..... for 10 minutes.

Ellie Holcomb
Bar Harbor, Maine

SUMMER GARDEN STEW

1 med. onion, sliced
1 clove of garlic, minced
1 tbsp. oil
4 or 5 fresh tomatoes, peeled, chopped
1 peeled eggplant, chopped, salted
1/2 green pepper, chopped
2 med. zucchini, sliced
1/2 lb. fresh mushrooms, sliced
1 tsp. oregano
Salt and pepper to taste

Saute ...... onion and garlic in oil in skillet until tender; drain.
Add .... tomatoes and 1/2 cup water.
Rinse ...... eggplant in cool water; drain.
Add .... eggplant and remaining vegetables to skillet.
Season ..... with salt and pepper.
Simmer ..... for 1 hour or until vegetables are tender, stirring occasionally.

Marianne M. Riddile
Fairfax, Virginia

VEGETABLE BEEF SOUP

1 c. cubed beef
1/2 c. chopped onion
1 can tomatoes, chopped
1/2 c. each chopped cabbage, celery, green pepper
1 tsp. artificial sweetener

Saute ...... beef with onion in skillet until brown.
Stir .... in remaining ingredients.
Simmer ..... until beef is tender.
Yields ...... 2 servings.

Frances Harper
Attica, New York

HEARTY PRESSURE COOKER WINTER SOUP

2 lb. beef chuck, cubed
Salt and pepper to taste
2 med. onions, coarsely chopped
3 lg. carrots, coarsely chopped
3 stalks celery, chopped
2 lg. potatoes, chopped
2 12-oz. cans vegetable juice cocktail

Saute ...... beef cubes in pressure cooker; drain.
Add .... remaining ingredients and 2 cups water, stirring to mix.
Cook .... at 15 pounds pressure for 10 minutes using pressure cooker instructions.
Yields ...... 8 servings.

Pat Church
Webb, Florida

CHILI WITH WAX BEANS

1 lb. lean ground beef
1/4 c. chopped onion
1 16-oz. can tomatoes
1 16-oz. can cut wax beans, drained
1 can tomato soup
1/4 tsp. pepper
Salt to taste
1 tsp. chili powder

Saute ...... ground beef and onion in skillet until brown; drain.
Add .... remaining ingredients.
Simmer ..... covered, for 30 minutes, stirring occasionally.
Yields ...... 6 servings.

Mrs. Elizabeth Richard
Lake Odessa, Michigan

SLIM CHILI

3 c. tomato juice
1 green pepper, chopped
1 tbsp. chopped onion
1/4 tsp. garlic powder
1 tbsp. chili powder
1 lb. ground beef, browned, drained
1 1-lb. can bean sprouts, drained

Combine .... first 6 ingredients in saucepan.
Simmer ..... covered, until thick, stirring occasionally.
Add .... bean sprouts.
Simmer ..... covered, for 15 minutes longer, stirring occasionally.

Martha Ann Webster
Malta Bend, Missouri

EASY CHICKEN SOUP

1 stewing chicken
3 tbsp. rice
Salt and pepper to taste
1 c. each chopped onion, celery, carrots
1 c. shredded cabbage
1 6-oz. package noodles

Boil .... chicken in water to cover in saucepan until tender.
Remove .... chicken from broth; cool slightly.
Place .... remaining ingredients in broth.
Simmer ..... until vegetables are tender.
Remove .... chicken from bone and chop.
Add .... to broth.
Simmer ..... for 15 minutes.
Yields ...... 10 to 12 servings.

Trinnie Minks
Ft. Scott, Kansas

RICH TURKEY VEGETABLE AND NOODLE SOUP

1 carrot, chopped
1 sm. onion, chopped
1 stalk celery, chopped
4 cloves
12 peppercorns
1 chicken bouillon cube
Salt
Bones of 1 cooked turkey
1 c. each sliced carrots, celery
1 c. chopped potatoes

1/4 c. chopped onion
1 10-oz. package frozen baby lima beans
1 c. noodles
2 c. chopped cooked turkey

Combine .... first 6 ingredients with 1 teaspoon salt, turkey bones and water to cover in large stock pot.
Simmer ..... for 3 hours.
Strain ...... and reserve 2 quarts broth.
Combine .... reserved broth with remaining ingredients and salt to taste in large saucepan.
Simmer ..... for 15 minutes.
Yields ...... 6 servings.

Photograph for this recipe on this page.

SALMON BISQUE

4 tbsp. butter, melted
4 tbsp. flour
3 c. milk
1 1/2 tsp. salt
1/2 tsp. paprika
1 c. canned tomatoes
1/2 c. chopped onion
2 tbsp. chopped parsley
1 1-lb. can pink salmon

Blend ...... butter and flour in saucepan.
Stir .... in milk gradually.
Cook .... until thickened, stirring constantly.
Add .... remaining ingredients and 2 cups water.
Simmer ..... for 20 minutes.

Janie Kent
Rome, Georgia

SHRIMP BISQUE

1/4 c. each finely chopped onion, celery
2 tbsp. flour
1 tsp. butter-flavored salt
1/4 tsp. paprika
Dash of white pepper
4 c. skim milk
14 oz. cooked shrimp, coarsely chopped

Combine .... first 2 ingredients with 1/4 cup water in saucepan.
Simmer ..... until vegetables are tender.
Add .... remaining ingredients except shrimp, mixing well.
Simmer ..... until thick, stirring constantly.
Fold .... in shrimp.
Heat .... to serving temperature.
Yields ...... 6 servings.

Carolyn Loup Auman
Thomasville, North Carolina

SEAFOOD GUMBO

1 1/2 c. tomato juice
1/4 c. cooked okra
1/4 c. chopped green pepper
1/2 c. chopped celery
2 tbsp. onion flakes
2 tsp. shrimp boil
1/4 tsp. garlic salt
Salt and pepper to taste
1/4 c. each cooked shrimp, crab

Boil .... tomato juice in saucepan until thick.
Add .... remaining ingredients except shrimp and crab.
Simmer ..... for 15 minutes.
Add .... shrimp and crab.
Heat .... to serving temperature.
Serve .... over rice.
Yields ...... 1 serving.

Gail Bumpus
Joshua, Texas

OYSTER STEW

2 c. oysters
4 c. milk, scalded
3 tbsp. butter
Salt and pepper
Paprika

Place .... oysters in saucepan with water to cover.
Simmer ..... until edges curl; drain.
Heat .... milk to scalding in saucepan.
Add .... oysters, butter and seasoning.
Yields ...... 6 servings.

Reena Belker
Fresno, California

sandwiches

FRUITY BAGELS

2 bagels, split, toasted
1 3-oz. package cream cheese, softened
Cinnamon, cloves to taste
1 peach, thinly sliced
1 banana, thinly sliced
Lemon juice
4 slices honeydew

Spread ..... bagels with cream cheese and sprinkle with cinnamon and cloves.
Dip .... peach and banana slices in lemon juice.
Layer ...... fruit slices over bagels.
Yields ...... 4 servings.

Charlene Gomez
Silver City, New Mexico

OPEN-FACED CRUNCHY SANDWICHES

1/4 c. vinegar
1 tsp. sugar
1/4 tsp. each salt, dillweed
Dash of pepper
1 lg. cucumber, thinly sliced
4 radishes, thinly sliced
4 slices bread, buttered

Combine .... first 5 ingredients in bowl.
Chill .... covered, for 3 hours or longer, stirring occasionally; drain.
Arrange ..... cucumber and radish slices on bread.
Yields ...... 4 servings.

Geneva Walton
Birmingham, Alabama

CARROT-CELERY SANDWICH SPREAD

4 med. carrots
1/2 green pepper
3 stalks celery
2 tbsp. chopped nuts
2 tbsp. wheat germ
1 tbsp. horseradish
3 tbsp. low-calorie mayonnaise
1 tsp. lemon juice
Salt to taste

Grind ...... first 5 ingredients together into bowl.
Add .... remaining ingredients, mixing well.
Spread ..... on Melba toast.
Yields ...... 2 cups.

Jean Passino
Keewatin, Minnesota

PEANUT BUTTER MIX

1 c. natural peanut butter
1/2 c. wheat germ

Combine .... peanut butter and wheat germ, mixing well.
Spread ..... on bread slices.

Myra Evans
West Alexandria, Ohio

BAKED SWISS CHEESE SANDWICHES

6 slices bread
3/4 c. dry white wine
2 eggs, well beaten
2 c. grated Swiss cheese
3 tbsp. butter

Arrange ..... bread slices in shallow baking dish.
Spoon ...... wine over bread, allowing to soak into bread.
Add .... eggs to cheese, mixing well.
Pour .... over bread.
Dot .... with butter.
Bake .... at 350 degrees until golden brown.
Yields ...... 4 to 6 servings.

Mrs. Lillian P. Dunbar
North Abington, Massachusetts

CHEESE-RAISIN SANDWICH FILLING

1/4 c. raisins
1 3-oz. package cream cheese, softened
1/4 c. peanut butter
1/4 c. chopped peanuts
1 tbsp. honey

Soak .... raisins in hot water to cover for 15 minutes; drain.
Chop .... raisins fine.
Combine .... raisins with remaining ingredients in bowl, mixing well.
Yields ...... 6 to 8 servings.

Tilly Dyer
Florissant, Missouri

PIMENTO-CHEESE SPREAD

1 4-oz. jar chopped pimentos
2 hard-boiled eggs, chopped
1/2 lb. hoop cheese, grated
3 tbsp. salad dressing
1/2 tsp. sugar
Salt to taste
2 tbsp. sour cream

Combine .... all ingredients in bowl, mixing well.
Chill .... for 30 minutes or longer.
Spread ..... on party rye bread slices.

Lola New
Beaumont, Texas

CHICKEN LITTLES

2 tbsp. flour
1 tbsp. sugar
1 tsp. dry mustard
1/2 tsp. salt
Dash of cayenne pepper
2 egg yolks, slightly beaten
3/4 c. skim milk
3 tbsp. vinegar
8 slices whole wheat bread
Watercress
Sliced chicken
1 can water chestnuts, drained, sliced

Mix .... first 5 ingredients in saucepan.
Stir .... in egg yolks and milk.

Cook . . . . over low heat until thick, stirring constantly.
Stir . . . . in vinegar.
Chill . . . . until serving time.
Spread . . . . . each slice of bread with dressing.
Layer . . . . . . several sprigs of watercress, chicken and several slices water chestnut on each slice.
Serve . . . . with remaining dressing.
Yields . . . . . . 8 servings.

Melanie Lawton
Claunch, New Mexico

HOT CHICKEN SALAD SANDWICHES

3/4 c. chopped canned chicken
3/4 c. celery slices
1/4 c. chopped walnuts
1 tbsp. minced onion
1 tbsp. lemon juice
1/3 c. mayonnaise
Salt and pepper to taste
4 slices bread
Butter

Combine . . . . first 7 ingredients in bowl, mixing well.
Toast . . . . . . bread on one side.
Butter . . . . . . untoasted side and spread with chicken mixture.
Place . . . . on baking sheet.
Bake . . . . at 425 degrees for 12 minutes.
Yields . . . . . . 4 servings.

Jenny Pitt
Warren, Michigan

TROPICAL CHICKEN SALAD SANDWICHES

2 c. chopped cooked chicken
1/2 c. chopped celery
Dash each of salt, pepper
1/4 c. chopped pecans
Low-calorie mayonnaise
6 hard rolls
6 slices canned pineapple
3 slices low-calorie cheese

Combine . . . . first 5 ingredients with enough mayonnaise to moisten in bowl, mixing well.

Cut . . . . slice from tops of rolls and scoop out centers, reserving shells.
Fill . . . . shells with chicken mixture.
Top . . . . each with pineapple slice and 1/2 slice cheese.
Place . . . . on broiler rack.
Broil . . . . until cheese melts.
Yields . . . . . . 6 servings.

Judy Light
Seattle, Washington

BEEFBURGERS ON RYE

1/2 lb. lean ground beef
4 slices rye bread, toasted
4 onion slices
8 tomato slices
Shredded mozzarella cheese

Divide . . . . . . ground beef into 4 portions.
Spread . . . . . on bread, covering to edges.
Place . . . . on rack in broiler pan.
Broil . . . . for 5 minutes or to desired doneness.
Top . . . . with onion and tomato slices and cheese.
Broil . . . . for 1 minute longer or until cheese melts.
Yields . . . . . . 4 servings.

Pam Freeman
Los Altos, California

SKINNY BURGERS

1 1/2 lb. ground beef
1 can consomme
1 tbsp. chopped onion
1 tsp. salt
1/8 tsp. pepper
2 tbsp. steak sauce
1/4 c. shredded carrot

Combine . . . . all ingredients in bowl, mixing well.
Shape . . . . . . into thin patties.
Place . . . . on broiler rack.
Broil . . . . to desired doneness.
Serve . . . . on toasted English muffin halves.
Garnish . . . . . with green pepper rings.
Yields . . . . . . 6 servings.

Mrs. Linda Hair
Austin, Texas

BUCKAROO SANDWICHES

1   4 1/2-oz. can deviled ham
1 egg, lightly beaten
1 c. shredded Cheddar cheese
6 slices raisin bread, toasted, buttered

Combine .... first 3 ingredients in bowl, mixing well.
Spread ..... on toast.
Broil .... until cheese melts.
Yields ...... 6 servings.

Cara Davis
Newcastle, Wyoming

HOT HAM AND CHEESE SANDWICHES

1/2 lb. Swiss cheese, shredded
1/2 lb. boiled ham, chopped
1/3 c. sliced green onion
2 hard-boiled eggs, chopped
1/2 c. chopped pimento
3 tbsp. mayonnaise
1/2 c. chili sauce
8 hot dog buns, split

Combine .... first 7 ingredients in bowl, mixing well.
Spread ..... on buns.
Wrap .... each bun in foil.
Bake .... at 400 degrees for 15 minutes.
Yields ...... 8 servings.

Queenie Johnson
Dubuque, Iowa

TROPICAL HAM AND CHEESE SANDWICHES

1   4 1/2-oz. can deviled ham
1 tbsp. brown mustard
2 tbsp. mayonnaise
1/4 c. finely chopped spicy green olives
2 tbsp. finely chopped green onion
1 tsp. finely chopped pickled green
    chili peppers
8 slices raisin bread
1   3-oz. package cream cheese, softened
2 tbsp. pineapple juice
1/4 c. chopped nuts
Salt to taste
4 pineapple slices, drained

Combine .... first 6 ingredients in bowl, mixing well.
Spread ..... over 4 slices bread.
Beat .... cream cheese with pineapple juice in small bowl until fluffy.
Stir .... in nuts and salt.
Spread ..... over remaining 4 slices bread.
Place .... each open-faced cream cheese sandwich on top of deviled ham sandwich.
Top .... with pineapple slice and garnish with maraschino cherries and mint sprigs.

Photograph for this recipe on page 17.

HAM AND CHEESE MELTS

4 slices white bread, toasted
2 tsp. prepared mustard
4 slices boiled ham
1   10-oz. package frozen asparagus spears, cooked, drained
1/2 c. shredded Swiss cheese
2 tbsp. each chopped green onion, pimento

Spread ..... toast with mustard.
Layer ...... ham and asparagus on toast.
Sprinkle .... with remaining ingredients.
Place .... on rack in broiler pan.
Broil .... for 3 minutes or until cheese melts.
Yields ...... 4 servings.

June Dawson
Boise, Idaho

HAM SURPRISE ROLLS

4 frankfurter buns, split
4 tsp. prepared mustard
1 c. shredded lettuce
1/4 c. chopped cucumber
2 tbsp. low-calorie French-style salad dressing
4 dill pickle strips
8 thin slices boiled ham

Spread ..... buns with mustard.
Combine .... lettuce, cucumber and salad dressing in bowl, mixing well.
Place .... 1/4 of the mixture and 1 pickle on end of 2 stacked ham slices.

Roll . . . . as for jelly roll, securing with toothpick.

Place . . . . in bun.

Lurlene Settles
Crete, Nebraska

SHRIMPBURGERS

3 tbsp. butter, melted
3 tbsp. flour
3/4 c. skim milk
12 oz. frozen shrimp, cooked, chopped
1 c. cooked rice
1/2 c. grated sharp Cheddar cheese
1 tbsp. instant minced onion
1 tsp. salt
1/8 tsp. pepper
1/2 tsp. curry powder
Fine dry bread crumbs

Blend . . . . . . butter and flour in saucepan.

Stir . . . . in milk gradually.

Cook . . . . until thick, stirring constantly.

Stir . . . . in shrimp, rice, cheese and seasonings.

Chill . . . . until firm enough to shape.

Shape . . . . . . into 6 patties.

Coat . . . . with crumbs.

Brown . . . . . . on both sides in oil in skillet.

Serve . . . . on whole wheat roll halves.

Yields . . . . . . 6 servings.

Abigail Moon
Los Angeles, California

TUNA BUNWICHES

1 c. cheese
1 can water-pack tuna, drained, flaked
3 hard-boiled eggs, chopped
2 tbsp. chopped onion
3 tbsp. chopped green pepper
2 tbsp. chopped stuffed olives
2 tbsp. chopped sweet pickles
1/2 c. mayonnaise
8 buns, split

Combine . . . . first 8 ingredients in bowl, mixing well.

Fill . . . . buns with mixture.

Wrap . . . . each in foil.

Bake . . . . at 250 degrees for 1/2 hour.

Yields . . . . . . 8 servings.

Connie Fields
Bingo, Florida

ZIPPY SALMON SANDWICHES

1 7 3/4-oz. can pink salmon, drained, flaked
1/3 c. low-calorie salad dressing
1 can water chestnuts, drained, finely chopped
1 tbsp. chopped onion
1 tsp. each soy sauce, lemon juice
6 slices whole wheat bread

Combine . . . . first 6 ingredients in bowl, mixing well.

Spread . . . . . on each bread slice.

Serve . . . . open-faced garnished with tomato and cucumber slices.

Yields . . . . . . 6 servings.

Paula Thomas
Bangor, Maine

beverages

INSTANT APPLE TINGLER

2 c. chilled apple juice
1 c. chilled grape juice
1 c. chilled orange juice
2 tbsp. lemon juice

Combine . . . . juices in 1-quart pitcher.

Serve . . . . over ice in tall glasses.

Laura Hill
Sparta, Tennessee

BANANA MILK SHAKE

1 lg. ripe banana, sliced
1 tbsp. sugar
1/2 c. crushed ice
1/2 tsp. vanilla extract
1/3 c. nonfat dry milk

Place . . . . banana and sugar in blender container.

Process . . . . . until smooth.

Add . . . . remaining ingredients and 1/2 cup cold water.

Process . . . . . until smooth and fluffy.

Pour . . . . into chilled glasses.

Yields . . . . . . 2 servings.

Mrs. Virginia Carlson
Port Allegany, Pennsylvania

CRANBERRY SLUSH

1 qt. cranberry juice
Grated rind and juice of 1 lemon and
    1 orange
Diet lemon-lime soda

Combine .... first 2 ingredients in freezer container.
Freeze ...... for 2 hours or until slushy.
Spoon ...... into glasses.
Pour .... soda over all to serve.

Amy Marvis
Maines, Pennsylvania

HOT GRAPEFRUIT TODDY

4 6-oz. cans frozen grapefruit juice
1/4 c. sugar
2 sticks cinnamon
2 tsp. whole cloves

Dilute ...... grapefruit juice in saucepan using package directions.
Add .... remaining ingredients.
Simmer ..... for 10 minutes.
Serve .... in mugs with cinnamon stick stirrers.
Yields ...... 12 servings.

Myra Gearson
Cary, North Carolina

 Drink liquids with meals to create a feeling of fullness.

LUSCIOUS SLUSH

1 20-oz. can unsweetened crushed pineapple
1 6-oz. can frozen unsweetened orange juice
1 med. banana, sliced
1 c. diet ginger ale

Combine .... first 3 ingredients in blender container.
Process ..... until blended.
Stir .... in ginger ale.
Pour .... into 9 x 13-inch freezer pan.
Freeze ...... for 30 minutes or until slushy.
Spoon ...... into glasses.

Annie M. Hart
Lakewood, Colorado

DIETER'S FRUIT DELIGHT

1 c. chilled pineapple juice
1/8 tsp. liquid non-calorie sweetener
1/3 c. instant dry milk powder
1 c. cracked ice
1/3 10-oz. package frozen strawberries

Combine .... all ingredients in blender container.
Process ..... at high speed until thick and foamy.
Serve .... in small glasses.
Yields ...... 6 servings.

Margaret Tisdale
Memphis, Tennessee

DYNAMIC DRINK

2 c. skim milk
Brewers yeast to taste
2 tbsp. lecithin granules
1 tbsp. safflower oil
1 tsp. vanilla extract
1 tbsp. honey

Combine .... all ingredients except honey in blender container.
Process ..... until smooth.
Chill .... overnight.
Stir .... in honey.

Mrs. Delphine Senn
Alexandria, Virginia

TASTER'S DELIGHT COCOA

1/4 c. cocoa
1/4 c. sugar
2 c. nonfat dry milk
1 c. evaporated skim milk
Dash of salt
1 tsp. vanilla extract

Combine .... cocoa and sugar with 1/2 cup water in 2-quart saucepan.
Boil .... for 1 minute, stirring constantly.
Mix .... dry milk with 1 cup water in bowl, blending until smooth.
Add .... to cocoa mixture with remaining ingredients and 4 cups water.
Heat .... to serving temperature.
Yields ...... 4 to 6 servings.

Marilyn Gornto
Perry, Georgia

salads

salads

AVOCADO RING WITH BLUEBERRIES

1 tsp. unflavored gelatin
1/2 tsp. sugar
1 tsp. salt
Pinch of pepper
2 med. ripe avocados, peeled, quartered
1 tsp. grated onion
1/2 tsp. lemon juice
1/4 tsp. grated lemon rind
1 c. yogurt
1/4 c. salad dressing
2 c. blueberries, rinsed, drained

Soften . . . . . . gelatin in 1/4 cup water in bowl.
Add . . . . next 3 ingredients and 1 cup boiling water, stirring to dissolve gelatin.
Force . . . . . . avocados through food grinder into large bowl.
Blend . . . . . . in next 3 ingredients.
Add . . . . gelatin mixture, yogurt and salad dressing, mixing well.
Spoon . . . . . . into ring mold.
Chill . . . . until firm.
Unmold . . . . on chilled plate.
Arrange . . . . . blueberries around edges and in center of ring.

Patricia Seay
Albert, Alabama

FRUIT SALAD SUPREME

6 c. strawberries
2 c. raspberries
1 lg. can unsweetened chunk pineapple, drained
1 lg. can unsweetened fruit cocktail, drained
2 c. mandarin oranges
5 bananas, sliced
1/2 lb. white grapes
Sugar substitute to taste

Combine . . . . all ingredients in serving bowl, mixing well.
Chill . . . . to serving temperature.
Yields . . . . . . 12-15 servings.

Diane Pratt
Atlanta, Georgia

CHEF'S FRUIT SALAD

1 head lettuce, chopped
1 c. cottage cheese
1 c. fresh pineapple chunks, drained
1/2 c. chopped apple
1/4 c. chopped walnuts
1/4 c. raisins
2 tbsp. French dressing
3 oranges, peeled, sectioned

Combine . . . . all ingredients in bowl, mixing well.
Chill . . . . . . to serving temperature.
Yields . . . . . . 6 to 8 servings.

Beverly Cawthorn
Baton Rouge, Louisiana

CANTALOUPE WALDORF SALAD

2 c. cubed cantaloupe
1 1/2 c. mandarin orange sections
3/4 c. halved seedless grapes
3/4 c. finely chopped celery
1/2 c. chopped nuts
1/2 c. chopped dates
Lettuce
Yogurt

Combine . . . . first 6 ingredients in bowl, mixing well.
Chill . . . . to serving temperature.
Serve . . . . on lettuce and top with yogurt.
Yields . . . . . . 6 servings.

Mary Dunn
Benson, Texas

MELON FRUIT SALAD

1 1/2 c. yogurt
1/3 c. maple syrup
3 tbsp. toasted sesame seed
1 tsp. grated orange rind
1/2 tsp. grated lemon rind
1/8 tsp. salt
1/2 watermelon
1 cantaloupe
1 honeydew melon
1 c. fresh blueberries

Combine . . . . first 6 ingredients in bowl, mixing well.
Chill . . . . covered, until serving time.
Cut . . . . watermelon, cantaloupe and honeydew melon with melon ball cutter.

Scoop . . . . . . out and discard remaining flesh from watermelon half.
Cut . . . . scallops around edge using 6-ounce juice can as pattern.
Arrange . . . . . melon balls and blueberries in shell.
Chill . . . . until serving time.
Spoon . . . . . . yogurt dressing over fruit before serving.
Yields . . . . . . 12 servings.

Linda Beau
Taylor, South Carolina

ORANGE-COT SALAD

1 lb. low-fat cottage cheese
1 can mandarin oranges, drained
1/2 c. coconut
1/2 c. pecans, finely chopped
1/2 c. yogurt

Combine . . . . all ingredients in bowl, mixing well.
Chill . . . . to serving temperature.
Yields . . . . . . 8-10 servings.

Faye Holley
Rochester, New York

TANGERINE SALAD

4 tangerines, peeled, seeded, sectioned
1 grapefruit, peeled, seeded, sectioned
1 unpeeled apple, cored, chopped
6 maraschino cherries, quartered
2 tbsp. cherry juice
2 tbsp. sugar
1 c. yogurt
1 lg. banana, sliced
Salad greens
1/4 c. sliced toasted almonds

Combine . . . . first 4 fruits in bowl, mixing well.
Blend . . . . . . cherry juice with sugar and yogurt in bowl.
Fold . . . . into fruit mixture.
Chill . . . . for 1 hour.
Add . . . . banana just before serving.
Arrange . . . . . on salad greens.
Sprinkle . . . . with almonds.

Betty Green
Chicago, Illinois

GOLDEN FRUIT SALAD MOLD

1 tbsp. gelatin
1 c. pineapple juice
1/4 c. sugar
Dash of salt
1/2 c. orange juice
1/4 c. mild vinegar
1 c. orange sections, diced

Soften . . . . . . gelatin in 1/4 cup water in bowl.
Heat . . . . pineapple juice in saucepan to boiling point.
Add . . . . to gelatin, stirring to dissolve.
Stir . . . . in next 4 ingredients.
Chill . . . . until partially set.
Fold . . . . in orange sections.
Spoon . . . . . . into mold.
Chill . . . . until set.
Yields . . . . . . 6 servings.

Ethel Harrington
New Haven, Connecticut

HIGH C SALAD

1 env. gelatin
2 tbsp. sugar
1/4 tsp. salt
1/2 c. orange juice
1 tbsp. lemon juice
1 tbsp. vinegar
2 drops of yellow food coloring
1 med. orange, sectioned, chopped
1 c. chopped cabbage
1/4 c. finely chopped celery

Combine . . . . gelatin, sugar and salt in medium saucepan, mixing well.
Stir . . . . in 1/2 cup cold water.
Cook . . . . over low heat until ingredients dissolve, stirring constantly.
Add . . . . juices, vinegar and food coloring with 3/4 cup water, mixing well.
Chill . . . . until thick.
Fold . . . . in remaining ingredients.
Pour . . . . into 3 1/2-cup mold.
Chill . . . . until firm.
Unmold . . . . onto serving plate.
Yields . . . . . . 6 servings.

Margaret McClean
Seattle, Washington

PINEAPPLE SALAD MOLD

1   20-oz. can juice packed crushed pineapple
1 bottle of low-calorie lemon-lime soda
1 env. unflavored gelatin
1 tbsp. lemon juice
Several drops of green food coloring
1   8 1/2-oz. can unsweetened grapefruit
    sections, drained, cut up
1/4 c. shredded cucumber, well drained

Drain ...... pineapple, reserving juice.
Add .... enough soda to reserved juice to
            measure 2 cups.
Soften ...... gelatin in 1/2 cup juice mixture
            in saucepan.
Simmer ..... until gelatin dissolves, stirring
            constantly.
Add .... remaining juice mixture, lemon
            juice and food coloring.
Chill .... until partially set.
Fold .... in remaining ingredients.
Pour .... into 4 1/2-cup mold.
Chill .... until set.
Unmold .... on salad greens.
Yields ...... 8 servings.

Jane Clammy
Ridgeway, Virginia

Make your own low-calorie salad
dressing by substituting water for a
portion of the oil.

SUGARLESS SALAD MOLD

1   8-oz. can unsweetened pineapple
1 tsp. vinegar
1 pkg. low-calorie gelatin dessert
2 tbsp. salad dressing
3/4 c. grated carrots

Drain ...... pineapple, reserving juice.
Add .... vinegar and enough water to
            juice to measure 7/8 cup.
Bring .... liquid to a boil in saucepan.
Add .... gelatin, stirring to dissolve.
Chill .... until thickened.
Add .... salad dressing, beating until
            frothy.
Stir .... in pineapple and carrots.
Pour .... into serving dish.
Chill .... until set.

Anna Patterson
Spray, North Carolina

FREEZE AND FORGET FRUIT SALAD

2/3 c. low-fat evaporated milk
1   8-oz. can unsweetened pears
1   8-oz. can unsweetened pineapple tidbits
1 egg, slightly beaten
1/4 c. sugar
Salt to taste
1 1/2 tbsp. flour
2 tbsp. vinegar
3 ripe bananas, mashed
1/2 c. chopped maraschino cherries
1 tbsp. lemon juice

Chill .... milk in shallow dish in freezer
            for 10 to 15 minutes until soft
            ice crystals form around edges.
Drain ...... pears and pineapple, reserving
            3/4 cup juice.
Combine .... reserved juice with next 5 ingre-
            dients in saucepan.
Cook .... until thickened, stirring con-
            stantly; cool.
Add .... fruit to mixture.
Beat .... chilled milk in mixer bowl at
            high speed for 1 minute or until
            stiff.
Add .... lemon juice.
Beat .... for 1 minute longer.
Fold .... into fruit mixture.
Spoon ...... into mold.
Freeze ...... for 5 to 6 hours or until firm.

Kathy Jones
Brook, Maine

FROZEN CHERRY SALAD

2 c. yogurt
2 tbsp. lemon juice
Sugar substitute to taste
1/8 tsp. salt
1   8-oz. can unsweetened crushed
    pineapple, drained
1 banana, diced
4 drops of red food coloring
1/4 c. chopped pecans
1   1-lb. can pitted Bing cherries,
    well drained

Combine .... first 6 ingredients in bowl with
            enough red food coloring to tint
            pink.
Fold .... in pecans and cherries.

Spoon . . . . . . into paper-lined muffin cups.
Cover . . . . . . with plastic wrap.
Freeze . . . . . until firm.
Thaw . . . . . . for 15 minutes before serving.
Peel . . . . off paper liners.
Serve . . . . on lettuce leaves.
Yields . . . . . . 12 servings.

Alice Patton
Decatur, Alabama

COMPANY CHICKEN SALAD

2 c. chopped cooked chicken
1 c. chopped celery
1 tbsp. lemon juice
Salt and pepper to taste
1 c. halved green grapes
1 c. pineapple chunks
1/2 c. almonds
Salad dressing

Combine . . . . all ingredients in salad bowl with enough salad dressing to moisten.
Chill . . . . to serving temperature.
Yields . . . . . . 6 servings.

Janice Benson
Chicago, Illinois

TOMATO STUFFED WITH PINEAPPLE-CHICKEN SALAD

3 tbsp. sugar
1/4 c. flour
1/2 tsp. salt
3/4 c. pineapple juice
2 egg yolks, beaten
1/4 c. lemon juice
1/3 c. instant nonfat dry milk
4 c. chopped cooked chicken
2 c. pineapple chunks
1 c. chopped celery
1/2 c. slivered almonds
1/2 c. chopped green pepper
8 med. tomatoes

Blend . . . . . . sugar, flour, salt and pineapple juice in saucepan.
Cook . . . . over low heat until thick, stirring constantly.

Stir . . . . a small amount of hot mixture into egg yolks; stir egg yolks into hot mixture.
Cook . . . . for 3 minutes longer, stirring constantly.
Stir . . . . in lemon juice.
Chill . . . . until serving time.
Dissolve . . . . dry milk in 1/3 cup ice water in bowl.
Beat . . . . until stiff.
Fold . . . . into chilled dressing.
Combine . . . . chicken with next 4 ingredients and 1 cup dressing in bowl, tossing to mix.
Cut . . . . stem ends from tomatoes and cut wedges to, but not through, bottom end.
Spoon . . . . . . chicken salad into tomatoes.
Top . . . . with additional dressing; garnish with pimento strips and olives.

Photograph for this recipe below.

SKINNY CHICKEN SALAD

2 c. slivered cooked chicken
1 c. diagonally sliced celery
1 clove of garlic, minced
1 tbsp. soy sauce
1 tsp. salt
1 tbsp. sesame seed oil
1 tsp. vinegar

Combine . . . . all ingredients in salad bowl, mixing well.
Chill . . . . to serving temperature.

Roberta Reins
Lawrence, Massachusetts

HEALTHFUL BEEF SALAD

2 c. sliced Chinese cabbage
1 1/2 c. cold roast beef, cut into
   thin strips
1 16-oz. can bean sprouts, drained
1 8-oz. can water chestnuts, drained,
   sliced
1 3/4 c. cooked rice
1 c. cooked peas
2/3 c. yogurt
1/3 c. mayonnaise
2 tbsp. soy sauce
1 tbsp. cider vinegar
1 tsp. celery seed
1/2 tsp. monosodium glutamate
1/4 tsp. each garlic salt, pepper

Combine .... first 6 ingredients in bowl, tossing to mix.
Chill .... in refrigerator.
Blend ...... remaining ingredients together in bowl.
Pour .... over beef mixture, tossing lightly.
Garnish ..... with pimento and green pepper strips.
Yields ...... 8 servings.

Sally Lee Thackery
High Point, North Carolina

HAM SALAD DELUXE

1/4 to 2/3 c. sugar
1 tsp. dry mustard
1 tsp. paprika
1 tsp. celery seed
1/4 tsp. salt
1/2 c. vinegar
1 tbsp. lemon juice
1 tsp. grated onion
1/3 c. honey
1 c. salad oil
1 avocado, sliced (opt.)
1 c. orange or grapefruit juice
2 c. grapefruit sections
1 c. orange sections
1 med. head lettuce, chopped
2 c. cooked ham strips
1 20-oz. can pineapple chunks, drained
1 c. sliced pitted ripe olives
1 c. celery slices

Combine .... first 8 ingredients in blender container.
Process ..... until mixed.
Add .... honey in fine stream, blending constantly.
Pour .... oil into mixture slowly, blending constantly.
Brush ...... avocado slices with orange juice.
Combine .... with remaining ingredients in large bowl.
Toss .... with enough honey dressing to moisten.

Sally New
San Diego, California

LAYERED HAM SALAD

2 env. gelatin
2 tbsp. sugar
Salt to taste
4 tbsp. lemon juice
1/4 c. vinegar
2 tbsp. chopped green pepper
2 c. finely shredded cabbage
3/4 c. mayonnaise
1/4 c. minced onion
1/2 c. chopped sweet pickle
1/2 c. diced celery
1 1/2 c. finely chopped ham

Combine .... 1 envelope gelatin, sugar and salt with 1/2 cup water in saucepan.
Cook .... over low heat until gelatin dissolves, stirring constantly.
Add .... 1 1/4 cups water, 2 tablespoons lemon juice and vinegar.
Chill .... until partially congealed.
Fold .... in green pepper and cabbage.
Pour .... into mold.
Chill .... until firm.
Combine .... 1 envelope gelatin, 2 tablespoons lemon juice, salt, mayonnaise and 1/2 cup water in saucepan.
Heat .... until gelatin dissolves, stirring constantly.
Chill .... until partially congealed.
Fold .... in remaining ingredients.
Spoon ...... over cabbage layer in mold.
Chill .... until set.
Unmold .... on salad greens.
Yields ...... 10 servings.

Leslie Holland
Middleton, Pennsylvania

SUMMER LAMB SALAD

1/4 c. each oil, vinegar
1 tbsp. each sugar, dried minced onion
1 tsp. each salt, oregano
1/4 tsp. pepper
3 c. chopped cooked lamb
2 c. each bite-sized pieces of lettuce,
endive, spinach
2 tomatoes, cut into wedges
2 hard-boiled eggs, sliced

Combine .... oil and vinegar with seasonings in large bowl.
Add .... lamb, tossing to coat.
Chill .... for 1 hour or longer.
Add .... remaining ingredients except eggs, tossing to mix.
Serve .... in lettuce-lined bowl garnished with egg slices.

Photograph for this recipe on page 27.

CRAB-FILLED AVOCADOS

2 avocados, chopped
Lemon juice
1 7 1/2-oz. can crab meat, flaked
1 5-oz. can water chestnuts, sliced
2 hard-boiled eggs, chopped
1/2 c. chopped cashews

Scoop ...... pulp from avocado halves; chop.
Combine .... with next 2 ingredients in bowl, tossing to mix.
Add .... water chestnuts, eggs and cashews, mixing well.
Spoon ...... mixture into avocado halves.
Chill .... in refrigerator.
Serve .... on lettuce leaves.
Top .... with low-calorie dressing.
Yields ...... 4 servings.

Marie Phillips
Franklin, Kentucky

CRAB AND GRAPEFRUIT SALAD

1 7-oz. can crab meat
1 c. diced celery
1/2 tsp. salt
1 tsp. onion salt
1/4 c. lemon juice
2 grapefruit sections
2 tomatoes, sliced into wedges

Combine .... first 5 ingredients in bowl.
Spoon ...... into center of serving plate.
Arrange ..... grapefruit sections and tomatoes alternately around crab meat mixture.
Yields ...... 4 servings.

Augusta Proctor
Adair, West Virginia

KING CRAB SALAD SUPREME

1/4 c. yogurt
1 tbsp. each chopped parsley, chives
1/2 tsp. Worcestershire sauce
1/4 tsp. lemon juice
1 7 1/2-oz. package frozen crab meat, drained
1/2 c. chopped cucumber
6 tomatoes, chopped
6 crisp lettuce cups
2 hard-boiled eggs, chopped

Combine .... first 6 ingredients in bowl, mixing well.
Add .... cucumber, tossing to mix.
Place .... tomatoes in lettuce cups on serving plate.
Spoon ...... crab mixture over tomatoes.
Sprinkle .... eggs over top.
Yields ...... 6 servings.

Wilma Bonnafur
Norfolk, Virginia

CRAB-STUFFED TOMATOES

4 tomatoes
1 6 1/2-oz. can crab meat, flaked
1/4 c. low-calorie salad dressing
2 tbsp. capers
2 tbsp. chopped celery
4 tsp. lemon juice
1/2 tsp. salt
1/4 tsp. pepper

Scoop ...... pulp from tomatoes, reserving shells.
Combine .... chopped pulp with remaining ingredients in bowl, mixing well.
Spoon ...... into tomato shells.
Yields ...... 4 servings.

Velma Marcus
Tucson, Arizona

MOLDED CRAB SALAD

2 env. unflavored gelatin
1 c. condensed beef broth
3 c. tomato juice
2 slices onion
2 bay leaves
1/4 tsp. celery salt
2 tbsp. lemon juice
1 c. chopped celery
1 7 1/2-oz. can crab meat, drained, flaked

Soften . . . . . . gelatin in 1/2 cup beef broth.
Combine . . . . tomato juice with next 3 ingredients in saucepan.
Bring . . . . to a boil; remove onion and bay leaves.
Stir . . . . in softened gelatin until dissolved.
Add . . . . remaining 1/2 cup broth and lemon juice.
Chill . . . . until partially set.
Fold . . . . in celery and crab meat.
Spoon . . . . . . into 5 1/2-cup mold.
Chill . . . . until firm.
Unmold . . . . onto serving plate.
Garnish . . . . . with hard-boiled egg slices.
Yields . . . . . . 6 servings.

Freddie Goins
Omaha, Nebraska

SEAFOOD COLESLAW

1 head cabbage, finely chopped
1 lb. carrots, finely chopped
1 can crushed pineapple, drained
1 can crab meat, flaked
1/2 lb. small shrimp, cooked
Salad dressing
Salt and pepper to taste
Pinch each of garlic salt, onion salt
1 tsp. sugar
2 tbsp. pineapple juice

Combine . . . . all ingredients in large bowl, mixing well.
Turn . . . . into serving bowl.
Garnish . . . . . with paprika.
Yields . . . . . . 6 servings.

Connie Betts
Ft. Meade, Maryland

SCALLOP-CHEESE SALAD

1 12-oz. package frozen scallops, cooked, chilled
6 c. mixed salad greens
3 hard-boiled eggs, sliced
1/2 c. chopped celery
4 oz. mozzarella cheese, shredded
1/3 c. low-calorie Italian salad dressing

Combine . . . . all ingredients except salad dressing in bowl, tossing to mix.
Chill . . . . for 1 hour or longer.
Serve . . . . with salad dressing.
Yields . . . . . . 6 servings.

Myrna Benson
Rockwell City, Iowa

FRUTTI TUNA SALAD

2 apples, coarsely chopped
4 c. shredded lettuce
1 lg. can water-pack tuna, drained, flaked
1 c. seedless grapes
Lemon juice and salt to taste
Low-calorie mayonnaise

Combine . . . . first 5 ingredients with enough mayonnaise to moisten in bowl, mixing well.
Serve . . . . in lettuce-lined bowls.
Yields . . . . . . 6 servings.

Verna Schlotmeier
Pickrell, Nebraska

SPRING TUNA SALAD

2 tbsp. finely chopped scallions
3 tbsp. chopped pitted ripe olives
2 c. salad greens
1 c. chopped celery
Dash of salt
2 6 1/2-oz. cans tuna, drained
1 1/2 tbsp. each chili sauce, French dressing, mayonnaise
4 lettuce cups
1 hard-boiled egg, sliced

Combine . . . . first 6 ingredients in bowl, mixing well.
Mix . . . . chili sauce, dressing and mayonnaise in small bowl, blending well.

Add . . . . dressing to salad, tossing lightly.
Chill . . . . to serving temperature.
Spoon . . . . . . salad into lettuce cups.
Top . . . . with egg slices.
Yields . . . . . . 4 servings.

Bari Thomas
Westland, Kansas

TUNA TOSS

1/2 head lettuce, chopped
1/2 cucumber, chopped
1 tomato, chopped
5 radishes, sliced
2 green onions, chopped
1/4 c. diced green pepper
1/2 avocado, cut into pieces
1 can tuna, drained
French dressing

Combine . . . . all ingredients with enough dressing to moisten in bowl.
Toss . . . . lightly to mix.
Yields . . . . . . 3-4 servings.

Joan Miller
Lincoln, Nebraska

TUNA VEGETABLE SLAW

1 7-oz. can tuna, drained
1/4 c. mayonnaise
1 tbsp. lemon juice
1 c. shredded cabbage
1 c. cooked peas
1/2 c. diced celery
1/2 c. chopped green peppers
1/4 c. shredded carrot
1 tbsp. chopped onion
1/4 tsp. salt

Break . . . . . . tuna into large chunks in bowl.
Combine . . . . mayonnaise and lemon juice in small bowl, mixing well.
Add . . . . remaining ingredients to tuna, mixing well.
Pour . . . . dressing over salad, tossing lightly.
Yields . . . . . . 4-6 servings.

Ruth Spring
Portland, Oregon

ASPARAGUS VINAIGRETTE

1/2 c. low-calorie Italian salad dressing
2 tbsp. dry Sauterne
2 tbsp. finely sliced green onion
2 tbsp. finely chopped green pepper
1 tbsp. finely snipped parsley
1 tbsp. drained pickle relish
1 10-oz. package frozen asparagus spears, cooked
2 sm. tomatoes, sliced

Combine . . . . first 6 ingredients in bowl, mixing well.
Arrange . . . . . asparagus in shallow dish.
Pour . . . . in marinade.
Marinate . . . . overnight in refrigerator, basting occasionally.
Drain . . . . . . reserving marinade.
Arrange . . . . . asparagus spears on lettuce leaves on individual salad plates.
Top . . . . with tomato slices.
Spoon . . . . . . a small amount of marinade over each serving.
Yields . . . . . . 4 servings.

Alice Brinkley
Danville, Virginia

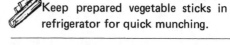 Keep prepared vegetable sticks in refrigerator for quick munching.

BEAN SPROUT SALAD

2 c. bean sprouts
2 green onions, finely chopped
1 clove of garlic, crushed
2 tsp. sesame seed
1 sm. red sweet pepper, chopped
Soy sauce to taste
1 tbsp. sesame seed oil
Vinegar to taste
Salt and pepper to taste

Remove . . . . tails from fresh bean sprouts.
Boil . . . . in water to cover in saucepan until slightly soft; drain.
Combine . . . . next 5 ingredients in bowl, mixing well.
Add . . . . bean sprouts and remaining ingredients, tossing lightly.
Chill . . . . well before serving.
Yields . . . . . . 4-6 servings.

Jerry Gunn
Waco, Texas

LOW-CALORIE THREE-BEAN SALAD

1 can French-cut green beans, drained
1 can wax beans, drained
1 can kidney beans, drained
1 med. onion, thinly sliced, separated
   in rings
1 med. green pepper, sliced
1 sm. jar pimento, chopped
Vinegar
Sugar substitute to taste

Combine .... vegetables in bowl, tossing to mix.
Add .... vinegar to cover and sugar substitute.
Chill .... covered, overnight; drain before serving.

Lynn Smith
Dona, Tennessee

MARINATED BEAN SALAD

2 c. French-style beans
2 to 3 tbsp. French dressing
3 tbsp. finely chopped onion
2 to 3 tbsp. grated Parmesan cheese

Combine .... first 3 ingredients in bowl, tossing well.
Chill .... for several hours, tossing occasionally.
Add .... cheese, tossing gently.
Garnish ..... with onion rings.

Flora Land
Quinn, Pennsylvania

BAVARIAN CABBAGE TOSS

1 2-lb. head red cabbage, shredded
2 tbsp. liquid sweetener
3 tbsp. low-calorie mayonnaise
1/2 tsp. salt
1/8 tsp. pepper
3 tbsp. lemon juice
2 tbsp. finely sliced green onions
2 sm. cucumbers, sliced diagonally

Combine .... cabbage and sweetener in large bowl, tossing lightly.
Chill .... for 1/2 hour; drain.
Combine .... next 4 ingredients in small bowl, blending well.

Pour .... over cabbage, mixing well.
Add .... remaining ingredients, tossing lightly to mix.

Joan Cookson
Denver, Colorado

FANCY COLESLAW

3 c. finely shredded cabbage
1 c. finely shredded carrots
1/4 c. chopped unpeeled apple
1/4 c. raisins
1/4 c. chopped walnuts
Bottled low-calorie coleslaw dressing

Combine .... all ingredients with enough dressing to moisten, mixing well.
Chill .... to serving temperature.
Yields ...... 6 servings.

Marge Flynn
Grand Falls, California

CARROT SALAD

1 lb. carrots, finely grated
1/4 c. honey
1/4 c. each chopped nuts, sunflower seeds

Combine .... all ingredients in bowl.
Toss .... to mix well.

Marie Houlk
Baldwin, Virginia

CHINESE VEGETABLE SALAD

1 can Chinese vegetables, drained
1 can seasoned green beans, drained
1 can sliced water chestnuts, drained
1 can sliced mushrooms, drained
1 can English peas, drained
1 1/2 c. chopped celery
Sliced onion to taste
1/2 c. sugar
3/4 c. wine tarragon vinegar

Combine .... first 7 ingredients in bowl, mixing well.
Combine .... sugar and vinegar in bowl, stirring to dissolve sugar.
Pour .... over vegetables, tossing to mix.
Chill .... overnight, stirring occasionally.
Yields ...... 12 servings.

Cally Hailey
St. Louis, Missouri

DILLED CUCUMBER SLICES

1 lg. cucumber
1/4 tsp. salt
Dash of pepper
1 sm. clove of garlic, crushed
1/8 tsp. dillweed
1/4 tsp. sugar
1 tbsp. lemon juice
1/2 c. yogurt
1 tsp. minced parsley

Score ...... cucumber lengthwise with fork.
Cut .... into thin slices.
Place .... in bowl and sprinkle with salt and pepper.
Chill .... covered, for 1 hour; drain.
Blend ...... remaining ingredients in bowl.
Fold .... into cucumber mixture.
Serve .... on salad greens.
Garnish ..... with parsley.
Yields ...... 4 servings.

Emily Younger
Leaks, Virginia

EGGPLANT SALAD

1 lg. eggplant, pierced
3 tomatoes, peeled, chopped
1 onion, peeled, chopped
2 tbsp. chopped fresh parsley
3 tbsp. olive oil
3 tbsp. cider vinegar
1 tsp. salt
1/2 tsp. pepper
Crisp lettuce

Place .... eggplant in baking dish.
Bake .... at 350 degrees for 1/2 hour; cool.
Peel .... and coarsely chop.
Combine .... with tomatoes in bowl, mixing well.
Combine .... next 6 ingredients in covered container, shaking to mix.
Add .... to eggplant mixture, tossing gently.
Serve .... on lettuce leaves.
Garnish ..... with tomato slices and ripe olives.
Yields ...... 6-8 servings.

Linda Crockett
Clarksdale, Missouri

JODIE'S LAYERED SALAD

2 c. each chopped lettuce, curly endive, romaine
1 med. red onion, thinly sliced
1 1/2 c. cooked peas, drained
1 c. julienne strips Swiss cheese
6 tbsp. mayonnaise
3 tbsp. sugar
Salt and pepper to taste

Layer ...... 1/3 of the vegetables, cheese and mayonnaise into bowl in order given.
Season ..... with 1 tablespoon sugar, salt and pepper.
Repeat ..... layers until all ingredients are used, seasoning each layer.
Chill .... covered for 2 hours.
Toss .... just before serving.
Garnish .... with crumbled bacon.
Yields ...... 6 servings.

Jodie Gray
Casey, Illinois

LOW-CALORIE MUSHROOM HEALTH SALAD

1 3/4-oz. package low-calorie lemon-flavored gelatin
1/4 tsp. salt
1/2 lb. fresh mushrooms
2 tbsp. lemon juice
1/2 c. chopped celery
2 tbsp. chopped cucumber
4 stuffed olives, thinly sliced
Lettuce leaves or watercress

Combine .... gelatin and salt with 3 1/2 cups boiling water in bowl, stirring to dissolve.
Chill .... until slightly thickened.
Rinse ...... mushrooms; drain.
Dip .... in lemon juice.
Add .... to gelatin with celery and cucumber, mixing well.
Pour .... into 6-cup mold.
Top .... with olive slices.
Chill .... until firm.
Unmold .... on lettuce leaves.
Yields ...... 6-8 servings.

Del Howard
Peona, Illinois

MARINATED MUSHROOM SALAD

6 tbsp. olive oil
3/4 c. dry white wine
1 1/2 tsp. salt
1/8 tsp. cayenne pepper
1/4 tsp. oregano
1/4 c. chopped fresh parsley
2 tbsp. chopped onion
3 tbsp. lemon juice
1 lb. fresh mushrooms, sliced

Combine .... first 8 ingredients in saucepan.
Simmer ..... for 15 minutes.
Marinate .... mushrooms in mixture in refrigerator several hours.
Arrange ..... on lettuce leaves.
Yields ...... 8 servings.

Boots McBride
Spray, North Carolina

ORIENTAL TOSS

1 head romaine, chopped
1 1-lb. can bean sprouts, drained
1 5-oz. can sliced water chestnuts
5 slices crisp-cooked bacon, crumbled
2 hard-boiled eggs, sliced
Salt and pepper to taste
1/2 c. salad oil
1/2 c. sugar
1/3 c. catsup
1/4 c. vinegar
2 tbsp. grated onion
2 tsp. Worcestershire sauce

Combine .... first 5 ingredients in bowl, mixing well.
Combine .... remaining ingredients in covered container, shaking to mix well.
Pour .... over salad, tossing to mix well.

Amy Eden
Burlington, North Carolina

FAVORITE MUSHROOM SALAD

2 tbsp. each Sherry, vinegar, oil
Dash each of dry mustard, sweet basil, tarragon
1 head romaine, torn into chunks
1 lb. fresh mushrooms, sliced

Combine .... first 6 ingredients in covered container, shaking to mix well.
Place .... romaine and mushrooms in large bowl.
Pour .... in dressing, tossing to mix.

Hannah Johnson
Jackson, Mississippi

MOCK POTATO SALAD

2 10-oz. packages frozen cauliflower, cooked, drained
2 stalks celery, chopped
1/2 green pepper, chopped
1 dill pickle, chopped
1 4-oz. can mushrooms, drained, chopped
3 tbsp. mustard
1 tbsp. onion flakes
1 tsp. parsley flakes
Salt to taste
1/2 tsp. Worcestershire sauce
1/2 tsp. lemon juice
Artificial sweetener to equal 2 tsp. sugar
2/3 c. buttermilk

Place .... cauliflower in blender container.
Process ..... until smooth.
Add .... remaining ingredients.
Process ..... until well blended.
Chill .... for several hours.
Yields ...... 4 servings.

Flo Gilette
Little Rock, Arkansas

SLIM POTATO SALAD

1 c. yogurt
1 c. creamed cottage cheese
2 tsp. mustard
2 tsp. seasoned salt
4 c. sliced cooked potatoes
1 c. sliced green onions and tops
1 c. sliced celery
1/2 c. diced green pepper
3 hard-boiled eggs, chopped
1 oz. blue cheese, crumbled

Combine .... first 4 ingredients in bowl, blending well.
Combine .... next 4 vegetables and eggs in large bowl, tossing gently to mix.

Add . . . . yogurt mixture, tossing gently.
Chill . . . . for several hours.
Fold . . . . in blue cheese just before
serving.
Yields . . . . . . 6-8 servings.

Alpha Fergus
Portland, Tennessee

FRESH SPINACH SALAD

1/4 c. vinegar
1 tbsp. sugar
Pinch of salt and pepper
1 bunch fresh spinach, washed, drained
2 strips crisp-fried bacon, crumbled
2 hard-boiled eggs, sliced

Combine . . . . vinegar, sugar, salt and pepper
with 1/2 cup water in saucepan.
Bring . . . . to a boil.
Pour . . . . over spinach in serving bowl.
Add . . . . bacon, tossing to mix.
Top . . . . with egg slices.
Serve . . . . immediately.

Bea Ellis
Kansas City, Missouri

JEWEL SALAD

1 tbsp. gelatin
1 tsp. horseradish
2 tbsp. lemon juice
2 tbsp. vinegar
2 tbsp. sugar
1/2 tsp. salt
1/2 c. diced celery
1/2 c. diced beets
1/2 c. finely shredded cabbage
1 tbsp. minced onion

Soften . . . . . . gelatin in 1/4 cup cold water in
bowl.
Add . . . . 1 1/4 cups boiling water, stirring
to dissolve.
Stir . . . . in next 5 ingredients.
Chill . . . . until mixture partially sets.
Fold . . . . in remaining vegetables.
Spoon . . . . . . into mold.
Chill . . . . until firm.
Unmold . . . . on lettuce leaves.

June Baxter
Waco, Texas

SURPRISE SALAD

1/2 c. salad dressing
1/2 c. low-calorie sweet and sour
French dressing
1 No. 2 can unsweetened pineapple chunks,
drained
2 cans bean sprouts, drained
1 3-oz. can chopped pimento, drained
2 sm. cans artichoke hearts, drained, sliced
1/2 tsp. salt

Blend . . . . . . salad dressing with French
dressing in bowl.
Combine . . . . remaining ingredients in bowl,
mixing well.
Add . . . . dressing, tossing to mix.
Serve . . . . on lettuce.
Garnish . . . . . with sliced hard-boiled eggs and
tomatoes.

Lessie Chambers
Beaver, Colorado

SUNSHINE ASPIC

1 1/2 c. tomato juice
1 bay leaf
1/4 tsp. each celery salt, onion salt
1 env. gelatin
2 tbsp. lemon juice
2 hard-boiled eggs, sliced

Combine . . . . 1 cup tomato juice, bay leaf,
celery salt and onion salt in
saucepan.
Simmer . . . . . for 5 minutes; remove bay leaf.
Soften . . . . . . gelatin in remaining tomato juice
in small bowl.
Stir . . . . into hot juice mixture until gela-
tin is dissolved.
Add . . . . 1/2 cup water and lemon juice,
mixing well.
Chill . . . . until thick.
Pour . . . . half the chilled mixture into
3 1/2-cup ring mold.
Arrange . . . . . egg slices around outer edge of
mold.
Pour . . . . remaining gelatin around and
over egg slices.
Chill . . . . until firm.
Unmold . . . . onto serving plate.
Yields . . . . . . 4 servings.

Tanya Campbell
Oklahoma City, Oklahoma

salad dressings

VERY BERRY-YOGURT DRESSING

1 c. yogurt
1/4 tsp. ground cinnamon
1 tbsp. sugar
1 c. sliced fresh strawberries

Combine . . . . all ingredients in blender container.
Process . . . . . until smooth.
Chill . . . . until serving time.
Serve . . . . over fresh fruit.
Yields . . . . . . 1 1/2 cups.

Lannette Baker
McCook, Nebraska

CREAMY FRUIT DRESSING

1/3 c. sugar
4 tsp. cornstarch
1/4 tsp. salt
Juice of 1 lemon
Juice of 1 orange
1 c. unsweetened pineapple juice
2 eggs, beaten
2 3-oz. packages cream cheese, softened

Combine . . . . first 6 ingredients in top of double boiler, mixing well.
Cook . . . . over hot water for 20 minutes, stirring constantly.
Stir . . . . a small amount of mixture into eggs; stir eggs into hot mixture.
Cook . . . . for 5 minutes longer, stirring constantly.
Add . . . . to cream cheese in mixer bowl.
Beat . . . . with electric mixer until well blended.
Chill . . . . in refrigerator.
Serve . . . . with fruit salad.
Yields . . . . . . 2 cups.

Virginia Worker
Coke, New York

LEMON-HONEY DRESSING FOR FRUIT SALAD

1 egg, beaten
1/4 c. lemon juice
1/2 c. honey
3 tbsp. milk
1 c. cottage cheese
Dash each of salt, mace

Combine . . . . first 3 ingredients in top of double boiler.
Cook . . . . over hot water until thickened, stirring constantly.
Combine . . . . remaining ingredients in mixer bowl.
Add . . . . hot mixture, beating with electric mixer until well blended.
Chill . . . . until serving time.

Hilda Green
Shearon, Texas

LOW-CHOLESTEROL COOKED SALAD DRESSING

1 tbsp. sugar
1/2 tsp. each dry mustard, paprika, salt
1/4 c. oil
2 tbsp. each white vinegar, lemon juice
2 tbsp. cornstarch

Combine . . . . first 7 ingredients in mixer bowl, blending well.
Mix . . . . cornstarch with 1 cup water in saucepan.
Simmer . . . . . until slightly thickened, stirring constantly.
Beat . . . . into oil mixture gradually with electric mixer until smooth.
Chill . . . . in refrigerator.
Yields . . . . . . 1 1/3 cups.

Elaine Horton
Early, New York

LEAN SALAD DRESSING

1/2 tsp. each salt, paprika, dry mustard, pepper
2 tsp. grated onion
2 tsp. chopped green pepper
1 c. tomato juice
2 tbsp. lemon juice

Combine . . . . all ingredients in jar.
Shake . . . . . . covered, until well blended.

Sissy Ellis
Salem, North Carolina

meats

GOURMET BEEF SKILLET

2 lb. beef sirloin tip, cut into
    2-in. strips
5 tbsp. butter, melted
1/2 c. dry Madeira wine
1 c. yogurt
3 tbsp. flour
1 tsp. paprika
1/2 tsp. salt
2 c. sliced mushrooms
1 green pepper, cut into strips
2 med. tomatoes, cut into wedges
1 1/2 tsp. fennel seed
1 8-oz. package noodles, cooked

Brown . . . . . . beef in 2 tablespoons butter in skillet.
Add . . . . wine.
Simmer . . . . . covered, for 1/2 hour or until tender.
Mix . . . . next 4 ingredients in bowl.
Add . . . . to beef mixture, stirring constantly.
Cook . . . . until thick, stirring constantly.
Add . . . . vegetables.
Simmer . . . . . covered, for 5 minutes.
Stir . . . . remaining 3 tablespoons butter and fennel seed into hot noodles.
Serve . . . . with beef and vegetables.
Yields . . . . . . 8 servings.

Photograph for this recipe on this page.

CHINESE PEPPER STEAK

1 lb. beef round steak, cut into sm. pieces
Dash of garlic powder
3 tbsp. soy sauce
1 tbsp. brown sugar
1 16-oz. can mixed Chinese vegetables, drained
1 16-oz. can tomatoes
2 green peppers, cut into lg. pieces
1 sm. onion, chopped
2 tbsp. cornstarch

Cook . . . . steak with next 3 ingredients in shortening in covered skillet over high heat for 5 minutes.
Add . . . . vegetables, mixing well.
Cook . . . . covered, over medium heat for 5 minutes longer.

Mix . . . . cornstarch with 1/4 cup cold water until smooth.
Add . . . . to steak mixture, stirring constantly.
Cook . . . . until thickened, stirring constantly.
Serve . . . . over rice.
Yields . . . . . . 4 servings.

Patty King
Canton, Ohio

OVEN SWISS STEAK

1 tsp. salt
1/4 tsp. pepper
1 2-lb. beef round steak, trimmed
1 med. onion, sliced
1 4-oz. can sliced mushrooms, drained
1 8-oz. can tomato sauce

Pound . . . . . . salt and pepper into steak with meat mallet.
Place . . . . in baking dish.
Top . . . . with onion and mushrooms.
Pour . . . . sauce over top.
Bake . . . . covered, at 350 degrees for 1 1/2 hours.
Bake . . . . uncovered for fifteen minutes longer, basting occasionally.
Spoon . . . . . . sauce over steak to serve.
Yields . . . . . . 8 servings.

Brenda Biffle
Fulton, Mississippi

RED BEEF STEW

3 lb. lean beef, cut into 1-in. cubes
2 cloves of garlic, minced
Corn oil
2 cans salt-free tomatoes, pureed
10 peppercorns, cracked
1/8 tsp. oregano
1/8 tsp. rosemary
6 sm. white onions
3 carrots, chopped
3 lg. potatoes, chopped
1/2 c. red wine

Trim . . . . fat from beef.
Saute . . . . . . beef and garlic in oil in large skillet.
Add . . . . 3 quarts water and next 4 ingredients.
Simmer . . . . . covered, for 1 hour.
Add . . . . vegetables.
Simmer . . . . . covered, for 1 3/4 hours longer.
Add . . . . wine.
Cook . . . . for 15 minutes longer.

Sally Rogers
Orlando, Florida

MARINATED BEEF FILETS

1/2 c. Claret
2 tbsp. soy sauce
1/2 c. finely chopped onion
2 tbsp. finely snipped parsley
1 clove of garlic, minced
Dash of pepper
4 4-oz. beef tenderloin filets,
   1 in. thick

Combine . . . . first 6 ingredients in plastic bag.
Add . . . . steaks, shaking to coat.
Marinate . . . . in refrigerator for 2 hours, turning occasionally.
Remove . . . . steaks, reserving marinade.
Place . . . . in broiler pan.
Broil . . . . 3 inches from heat source for 13 minutes or to desired degree of doneness, turning once.
Heat . . . . reserved marinade to boiling point in saucepan.
Spoon . . . . . . over broiled steak.
Yields . . . . . . 4 servings.

Judy West
Fresno, California

MARINATED BEEF KABOBS

1/2 env. dry onion soup mix
1 beef bouillon cube
1 tsp. prepared horseradish
1/4 tsp. paprika
1 lb. beef sirloin, cubed
12 lg. fresh mushrooms
2 med. tomatoes, cut into wedges

Combine . . . . first 4 ingredients with 3/4 cup water in saucepan.
Simmer . . . . . for 5 minutes; cool.
Add . . . . steak and mushrooms, mixing well
Marinate . . . . covered, in refrigerator for several hours.
Drain . . . . . . steak, reserving marinade.
Alternate . . . steak, mushrooms and tomatoes on skewers.
Broil . . . . over hot coals for 9 to 11 minutes, turning once and brushing with marinade occasionally.
Yields . . . . . . 4 servings.

Donnie Evans
Norfolk, Virginia

 Omit salt in cooking; season lightly to taste at the table.

EASY STROGANOFF FOR ONE

1 8-oz. minute steak, cut in strips
2 tsp. onion flakes
1/2 env. instant chicken broth mix
1/2 tsp. garlic powder
2 tbsp. catsup
3/4 tsp. Worcestershire sauce
1/2 c. sliced mushrooms
1/4 c. evaporated skim milk
1/2 c. cooked noodles

Stir-fry . . . . . steak in nonstick skillet until brown.
Add . . . . next 5 ingredients with 1/2 cup hot water, mixing well.
Simmer . . . . . for 10 minutes.
Stir . . . . in mushrooms and milk.
Heat . . . . to serving temperature.
Serve . . . . over noodles.
Yields . . . . . . 1 serving.

C. C. Davis
Stevens Point, Wisconsin

STEAK AND SPINACH STIR FRY

1/2 lb. flank steak, thinly sliced
   diagonally
2 tbsp. oil
1/2 tsp. salt
2 tsp. soy sauce
1 1/2 lb. spinach, coarsely chopped
1 tbsp. cornstarch
1 c. chicken broth

Stir-fry ..... steak in hot oil in skillet for 2 minutes.
Sprinkle .... with salt and soy sauce; remove from skillet.
Stir-fry ..... spinach in pan drippings for 2 minutes.
Add .... cornstarch blended with broth, stirring until smooth.
Cook .... until thick, stirring constantly.
Stir .... in steak.
Cook ...... until heated through.
Serve .... over rice.

Philene Caswell
Green River, Utah

STUFFED FLANK STEAK

1/2 green pepper, chopped
4 oz. chopped onion
4 oz. mushrooms
1 clove of garlic, minced
1 chicken bouillon cube
1 8-oz. beef flank steak
Garlic powder

Combine .... first 5 ingredients with 1/4 cup water in saucepan.
Simmer ..... until vegetables are tender.
Spread ..... vegetables over steak.
Roll .... and secure with skewer.
Sprinkle .... roll with garlic powder.
Place .... on rack in baking pan.
Bake .... at 350 degrees for 1 hour or until tender.

Laura Johnson
Denver, Colorado

BARBECUED CHUCK ROAST

1/3 c. wine vinegar
1/4 c. catsup
2 tbsp. soy sauce
1 tsp. mustard
1/4 tsp. each garlic powder, pepper
2 tsp. salt
1 3-lb. 2-in. thick chuck roast, trimmed

Combine .... first 7 ingredients in small bowl.
Pour .... over roast in shallow pan.
Let .... stand, covered, for 3 hours at room temperature, turning occasionally.
Drain ...... reserving marinade.
Place .... on rack in broiler pan.
Broil .... 6 inches from heat source for 1 hour or to desired doneness, turning and basting frequently with reserved marinade.
Yields ...... 8 servings.

Belenda Johnson
Mason City, Iowa

NEW WORLD BEEF POT ROAST

1 16-oz. can whole tomatoes
1 3 1/2 to 4-lb. beef blade roast
1/4 c. flour
1 1/2 tsp. salt
1/4 tsp. pepper
2 tbsp. oil
1/2 tsp. aniseed
1 clove of garlic, crushed
1 beef bouillon cube
1 med. onion, chopped
1 14 1/2-oz. can artichoke hearts, drained, halved
1 6-oz. can pitted ripe olives, drained

Drain ...... tomatoes, reserving liquid.
Coat .... roast with flour seasoned with salt and pepper, reserving excess flour.
Brown ...... roast in oil in large skillet; drain.
Add .... aniseed, garlic and bouillon cube dissolved in 1/3 cup hot water.
Cook .... covered, for 1 1/4 hours; turn roast.
Add .... onion and tomato liquid.
Cook .... covered, for 1 hour longer.
Add .... tomatoes, artichoke hearts and olives.
Cook .... for 10 minutes longer.
Remove .... roast and vegetables to heated serving platter.
Stir .... reserved seasoned flour into 1/4 cup cold water.

Add .... to pan drippings.
Cook .... until thick, stirring constantly.
Serve .... gravy with roast.

Photograph for this recipe on page 41.

MICROWAVE HAMBURGER STROGANOFF

1 lb. ground beef
1/2 lb. fresh mushrooms, sliced
1 med. onion, chopped
3 tbsp. flour
2 tsp. instant beef bouillon
1/2 tsp. salt
1/2 tsp. prepared mustard
1/8 tsp. pepper
1/2 c. buttermilk
2 tsp. dried parsley

Crumble .... ground beef into 1 1/2-quart glass casserole.
Sprinkle .... with mushrooms and onion.
Microwave .. on High for 7 or 8 minutes, stirring twice; drain.
Stir .... in next 5 ingredients with 1 cup water, mixing well.
Microwave .. covered, on High for 7 minutes, stirring once.
Stir .... in buttermilk and parsley flakes.
Microwave .. covered, for 2 or 3 minutes or until hot.
Yields ...... 4 servings.

Karen Williams
Elk River, Minnesota

JUICY MEAT LOAF

3/4 lb. lean ground beef
1/3 c. soft bread crumbs
3 tbsp. finely chopped onion
1/3 c. drained canned tomatoes
Dash of pepper
1/2 c. instant dry milk

Combine .... all ingredients in bowl, mixing well.
Shape ...... into loaf.
Place .... in shallow pan.
Bake .... at 350 degrees for 1 hour or until brown.
Yields ...... 4 servings.

Esta Newman
Bluffs, Illinois

BERRY BURGERS

1 lb. lean ground beef
1 tbsp. finely chopped onion
1/2 tsp. salt
1/4 tsp. pepper
1 tbsp. cornstarch
1 tbsp. sugar
3/4 c. low-calorie cranberry juice
2 tsp. lemon juice

Combine .... ground beef, onion, salt and pepper in bowl, mixing well.
Shape ...... into 4 thick patties.
Broil .... to desired doneness.
Combine .... cornstarch and sugar in saucepan.
Stir .... in cranberry juice gradually.
Cook .... until thick, stirring constantly.
Stir .... in lemon juice.
Spoon ...... over patties.
Yields ...... 4 servings.

Betty Bellows
Santa Rosa, California

CHEESEBURGER-STUFFED PEPPERS

8 green peppers
1 lb. lean ground beef
1/4 c. chopped onion
1 1/2 c. dry bread crumbs
1 c. shredded mozzarella cheese
1 c. chopped mushrooms
2 med. tomatoes, chopped
1/2 tsp. Worcestershire sauce
Salt to taste

Cut .... tops from peppers, removing seeds.
Brown ...... ground beef with onion in skillet, stirring until crumbly; drain.
Stir .... in remaining ingredients, reserving half the cheese.
Spoon ...... into peppers in baking dish.
Bake .... covered, at 350 degrees for 25 minutes.
Sprinkle .... with reserved cheese.
Bake .... for 5 minutes longer until cheese melts.
Yields ...... 8 servings.

Sally Pepperdine
Riverside, California

MICROWAVE SALISBURY STEAK

1 1/2 lb. ground beef
1/2 c. oatmeal
1/4 c. chopped green pepper
1 tsp. dried parsley
1 egg
1/2 tsp. garlic powder
1/4 tsp. pepper
1 can onion soup
1 2-oz. can sliced mushrooms
1/3 c. catsup
1 tbsp. cornstarch
1/4 tsp. basil
1 tsp. Worcestershire sauce

Combine .... first 7 ingredients in bowl, mixing well.
Shape ...... into patties.
Place .... in 6 x 10-inch glass baking dish.
Microwave .. covered, on Roast for 5 minutes.
Combine .... remaining ingredients in bowl, mixing well.
Pour .... over patties.
Cook .... covered, for 8 to 10 minutes longer or to desired degree of doneness.
Let .... stand, covered, for 5 minutes.
Yields ...... 6 servings.

Marilynn Collins
Bridgeport, Texas

MICROWAVE SPINACH LASAGNA

1 lb. ground beef
1 6-oz. can tomato sauce
1/4 c. minced onion
1 tsp. sweet basil
1 tsp. parsley flakes
1/4 tsp. oregano
Dash of garlic salt
Dash of pepper
1 4-oz. can sliced mushrooms, drained
1 10-oz. package frozen chopped spinach
8 oz. cottage cheese
4 oz. mozzarella cheese, sliced

Crumble .... ground beef into glass casserole.
Microwave .. on High for 6 minutes.
Stir .... in next 8 ingredients, mixing well.
Microwave .. spinach on High for 3 minutes.
Mix .... spinach with cottage cheese in bowl.

Layer ...... half the spinach mixture, beef mixture and mozzarella cheese into baking dish.
Repeat ..... layers.
Microwave .. on Medium for 12 minutes or until bubbly.
Yields ...... 4 servings.

Sharon Sharp
Richardson, Texas

HAM AND VEGETABLE BAKE

2 med. onions, sliced
1 c. green beans
1/2 c. whole kernel corn
2 1/2 c. canned tomatoes
2 c. cubed cooked ham
1/4 c. uncooked long grain rice
1/2 tsp. pepper
1 tsp. sugar

Combine .... all ingredients in 2-quart casserole, mixing well.
Bake .... covered, at 350 degrees for 1 hour.

Mable Gunn
Macon, Georgia

HEARTY HAM AND LENTIL BAKE

2 c. dried lentils
1 onion, chopped
2 bay leaves
2 c. chopped cooked ham
1/2 tsp. dried thyme
1/2 tsp. dried marjoram
1/2 tsp. pepper
6 carrots, cut into chunks
1 8-oz. can tomato sauce
Salt to taste

Combine .... lentils, onion, bay leaves and 1 quart water in saucepan.
Simmer ..... covered, for 30 minutes; drain.
Combine .... lentils with remaining ingredients in 2-quart casserole, mixing well.
Bake .... covered, at 350 degrees for 1 1/2 hours.
Bake .... uncovered, 15 minutes longer.
Yields ...... 6 servings.

Donna Moss
Cheyenne, Wyoming

STIR-FRIED HAM AND CABBAGE

1 sm. head cabbage, chopped
Oil
1/2 c. chopped cooked ham
1/4 c. chopped green onion with tops
2 tbsp. chopped parsley
1 clove of garlic, minced
1 chicken bouillon cube
1/2 tsp. salt

Stir-fry ..... cabbage in small amount of hot oil in large skillet for 1 minute.
Add .... remaining ingredients with 1/2 cup water, mixing well.
Simmer ..... covered, for 5 minutes.
Cook .... uncovered, until cabbage is tender-crisp.

Grace Bell
Carson, Nevada

GLAZED LAMB CHOPS

8 3/4-in. thick lamb chops, trimmed
Salt to taste
1/4 c. low-calorie marmalade
2 tsp. lemon juice

Sprinkle .... lamb chops with salt.
Place .... in broiler pan.
Broil .... 4 inches from heat source for 12 minutes, turning once.
Combine .... marmalade and lemon juice in bowl.
Spread ..... over chops.
Broil .... for 4 to 6 minutes longer or to desired degree of doneness.
Garnish ..... with fresh orange slices.
Yields ...... 4 servings.

Judy Macon
Erwin, Tennessee

ZESTY LIVER WITH MUSHROOMS

1 4-oz. can mushrooms, drained
1/3 c. low-calorie French dressing
1 lb. calf liver

Combine .... mushrooms and salad dressing in small bowl.
Let .... stand for 30 minutes, stirring frequently.
Drain ...... reserving marinade.
Cut .... liver into serving pieces.

Coat .... liver with reserved marinade and place on rack in broiler pan.
Broil .... 3 inches from heat source for 4 minutes; turn and top with mushrooms.
Broil .... to desired doneness.
Yields ...... 4 servings.

Candace Peterson
Hinckley, Ohio

PORK AND CARROT LOAF

1 1/2 c. ground carrots
1 1/2 c. bread crumbs
1 c. ground cooked pork
2 eggs
1 1/2 c. canned tomatoes
1 1/2 tsp. salt
1/4 tsp. pepper
2 tbsp. minced onion

Combine .... all ingredients in bowl, mixing well.
Pour .... into well-oiled loaf pan.
Bake .... at 350 degrees for 1 hour or until lightly browned.
Yields ...... 6 servings.

Doris Baker
Jonesboro, Arkansas

PORK CHOW MEIN

2 onions, sliced
2 c. sliced celery
1 tbsp. vegetable oil
2 c. diced cooked pork
1 tbsp. molasses
5 tbsp. soy sauce
1 19-oz. can bean sprouts, drained
3 tbsp. cornstarch

Saute ...... onions and celery in oil in skillet for 5 minutes.
Add .... pork, molasses, soy sauce and 2 cups water, mixing well.
Simmer ..... for 15 minutes.
Stir .... in bean sprouts.
Mix .... cornstarch with 1/4 cup water.
Stir .... into pork mixture.
Cook .... until thickened, stirring constantly.
Yields ...... 4 servings.

Norma Zimmerman
White Plains, New York

SWEET AND SOUR PORK

2 lb. lean pork, cut into thin strips
1 tbsp. oil
1 c. chicken bouillon
2 tsp. soy sauce
1/4 green pepper, cut in strips
1/4 onion, chopped
1/4 c. packed brown sugar
2 slices canned pineapple, cut in wedges
1/2 c. pineapple juice
1/2 c. blanched whole almonds
1/4 c. vinegar
1/4 c. sugar
2 tsp. cornstarch

Saute ...... pork in hot oil in skillet until brown.
Cook .... covered, for 10 minutes.
Add .... next 10 ingredients.
Simmer ..... for 5 minutes.
Stir .... in cornstarch mixed with 1/4 cup cold water.
Simmer ..... over low heat until thickened, stirring constantly.
Serve .... over rice.
Yields ...... 4-6 servings.

Judy Jones
Norfolk, Virginia

ARABIAN PORK CHOPS

4 pork chops
2 onions, sliced
2 tomatoes, sliced
2 tbsp. chopped green pepper
1 tbsp. flour
Salt to taste

Brown ...... pork chops on both sides in oil in skillet.
Place .... in casserole.
Layer ...... vegetables on top.
Stir .... flour and salt into pan drippings.
Add .... 1 cup water gradually, mixing well.
Cook .... until thick, stirring constantly.
Pour .... over chops.
Bake .... covered, at 350 degrees for 1 1/4 hours.

Anne Campbell
Lamont, Michigan

BAKED PORK CHOPS WITH ORANGE SAUCE

3/4 c. orange juice
1 tbsp. brown sugar
1 tsp. salt
1/2 tsp. cloves
1/4 tsp. pepper
4 1-in. thick pork chops
2 tbsp. grated orange rind
1 tbsp. oil
2 oranges, cut into 1/2-in. slices

Blend ...... orange juice, brown sugar, salt, cloves and pepper in shallow dish.
Add .... pork chops, turning to coat.
Sprinkle .... with orange rind.
Chill .... covered, for several hours.
Drain ...... chops, reserving marinade.
Brown ...... chops in oil in skillet.
Place .... in baking dish.
Pour .... reserved marinade over top.
Bake .... at 350 degrees for 1 hour.
Arrange ..... orange slices over chops.
Bake .... until heated through.
Yields ...... 4 servings.

Photograph for this recipe above.

 Try eating meals on a smaller plate.

MAKE-AHEAD PORK CHOP CASSEROLE

4 pork chops
3/4 c. rice
1 onion, sliced
1 tomato, sliced
1 bell pepper, sliced into rings
1 can beef bouillon

Saute ...... pork chops in skillet until brown.
Place .... rice in casserole.
Layer ...... pork chops and vegetables over rice.
Pour .... bouillon over top.
Bake .... at 375 degrees for 1 hour or until pork chops are tender, adding water if necessary.

Carole James
San Mateo, California

BROILED PORK CHOPS IN MARINADE

1 onion, minced
1 clove of garlic, chopped
1/2 c. soy sauce
1 tbsp. ginger
3 tbsp. sugar
8 2-in. thick pork chops

Combine .... first 5 ingredients with 2/3 cup water in large dish, mixing well.
Add .... pork chops, turning to coat.
Marinate .... for 10 hours or longer in refrigerator.
Place .... on rack over hot coals.
Cook .... until done.
Yields ...... 8 servings.

Deana Shute
Lesterville, Louisiana

CRANBERRY PORK CHOPS

6 pork chops
1/2 tsp. salt
4 c. ground cranberries
1 apple, ground
3/4 c. honey
1/2 tsp. cloves

Brown ...... pork chops on both sides in skillet.
Combine .... remaining ingredients in bowl, mixing well.
Layer ...... half the pork chops and cranberry mixture in baking dish.
Repeat ..... layers with remaining ingredients.
Bake .... covered, at 350 degrees for 1 hour.

Jodie Robertson
Umbrella Point, New Jersey

CREOLE PORK CHOPS

4 pork chops
Salt and pepper to taste
1 tbsp. oil
1/2 tsp. celery seed
3 tbsp. vinegar
1/4 tsp. ginger
1 tsp. sugar
1 tsp. flour
1/3 c. catsup

Sprinkle .... pork chops with salt and pepper.
Brown ...... on both sides in oil in skillet.
Combine .... remaining ingredients and 1/2 cup water in bowl, mixing well.
Pour .... over pork chops.
Bake .... at 325 degrees for 1 hour; turn chops.
Bake .... for 30 minutes longer.

Flo Gordon
Hampson, Pennsylvania

SLOW COOKING PORK CHOPS

6 pork chops
2 cans French-cut green beans
2 8-oz. cans tomato sauce
1/2 c. chopped green pepper
1 clove of garlic, chopped
1 med. onion, chopped

Saute ...... pork chops in skillet until brown.
Place .... remaining ingredients in slow cooker.
Add .... pork chops and enough water to almost cover chops.
Cook .... on Low for 6 to 8 hours or until pork chops are tender.

Marcia Cook
Beaumont, Texas

SPICY PORK CHOP CASSEROLE

6 3/4-in. thick pork chops
3 tbsp. oil
1 lg. onion, cut into 6 slices
2 tsp. chili powder
1 green pepper, chopped
1 c. rice
1 8-oz. can tomato sauce
Salt to taste

Brown . . . . . . pork chops on both sides in oil in skillet; remove from skillet.
Saute . . . . . . onion in pan drippings until brown; remove from skillet.
Stir . . . . chili powder into pan drippings.
Cook . . . . for 2 minutes.
Add . . . . green pepper, rice, tomato sauce, salt and 1 1/4 cups water.
Bring . . . . to a boil.
Pour . . . . into shallow 2-quart baking dish.
Arrange . . . . . pork chops in baking dish.
Top . . . . each chop with onion slices.
Bake . . . . covered, at 375 degrees for 1 hour.

Claudia Marshall
Pittsburgh, Pennsylvania

VEAL BIRDS

1 1/2 lb. veal cutlets, sliced thin
Salt and pepper to taste
2/3 c. finely chopped celery
2/3 c. finely grated carrots
2 tbsp. minced parsley
1 c. chopped onions
1 1/2 c. beef bouillon

Cut . . . . veal into 6 slices.
Sprinkle . . . . with salt and pepper.
Combine . . . . next 3 ingredients with 1/2 cup onions in bowl, mixing well.
Spoon . . . . . . 1/6 of the vegetable mixture onto each veal slice.
Roll . . . . and secure with toothpicks.
Arrange . . . . . rolls in baking dish.
Sprinkle . . . . with remaining onions.
Bake . . . . at 425 degrees for 30 minutes or until golden brown.
Pour . . . . beef bouillon over rolls.
Bake . . . . at 350 degrees for 45 minutes longer or until tender.

Maxine Joseph
Green Bay, Wisconsin

MICROWAVE VEAL DISH

1 beef bouillon cube
1 c. bulgur wheat
1 8 1/2-oz. can sliced water chestnuts
2 lb. veal cubes
1 c. chopped celery
1/3 c. undrained mushrooms
1 med. onion, chopped
1 can golden mushroom soup
1 tsp. salt

Dissolve . . . . bouillon cube in 2 cups hot water in saucepan.
Stir . . . . in bulgar wheat.
Simmer . . . . . covered, for 15 minutes.
Add . . . . remaining ingredients and 1 1/2 cups water, mixing well.
Place . . . . in casserole.
Microwave . . covered, on High for 20 minutes, stirring once.

May substitute wild rice for bulgar wheat.

Sue Black
Condon, Oregon

STUFFED GREEN PEPPERS

4 green peppers
1 1/2 c. finely ground veal
1/2 onion, chopped
1 c. cooked rice
2 tomatoes, chopped
2 hard-boiled eggs, chopped
2 tbsp. chopped pimento
Salt and pepper to taste
1/4 c. Parmesan cheese

Cut . . . . 3 peppers in half lengthwise, removing seeds.
Cook . . . . for 4 minutes in boiling salted water in saucepan.
Saute . . . . . . veal with remaining chopped pepper and onion in skillet until brown; drain.
Combine . . . . veal mixture with remaining ingredients except cheese in bowl, mixing well.
Stuff . . . . pepper halves with mixture.
Sprinkle . . . . with cheese.
Place . . . . in baking pan.
Bake . . . . at 400 degrees for 30 minutes or until peppers are tender.

Sue Howard
Oshkosh, Wisconsin

seafood

BAKED FISH MEDITERRANEAN

1 c. finely chopped onion
1 clove of garlic, minced
1/2 c. chopped celery
1 15-oz. can tomato sauce
1/8 tsp. ground cloves
1 bay leaf
1 1/2 c. shredded carrots
3/4 c. chicken broth
Salt and pepper to taste
2 lb. fish fillets

Saute . . . . . . onion, garlic and celery in skillet until tender.
Add . . . . remaining ingredients except fish.
Simmer . . . . . covered, for 30 minutes, stirring occasionally.
Roll . . . . up fish, securing with pick.
Arrange . . . . . in greased shallow baking dish.
Cover . . . . . . with sauce.
Bake . . . . at 350 degrees for 35 minutes or until fish flakes easily.
Garnish . . . . . with parsley.

Mrs. Carol Lovett
Costa Mesa, California

BARBECUED CATFISH

6 med. catfish
1 tsp. Worcestershire sauce
1/8 tsp. paprika
1/2 c. oil
1/4 c. each white vinegar, catsup
2 tbsp. sugar
1/4 tsp. each salt, pepper

Fillet . . . . and skin catfish.
Combine . . . . all ingredients except catfish in bowl, mixing well.
Pour . . . . marinade over catfish in shallow dish.
Let . . . . stand for 20 minutes.
Drain . . . . . . reserving marinade.
Cook . . . . 4 inches above hot coals on greased grill for 5 minutes on each side or until fish tests done, basting frequently with reserved marinade.

Cynthia Evers
Paducah, Kentucky

LOW-CAL ITALIAN COD

4 cod fillets
Salt, pepper, garlic powder to taste
1 c. each chopped onion, green pepper
1 can stewed tomatoes
Oregano to taste

Place . . . . cod in baking dish.
Layer . . . . . . remaining ingredients in order given over cod.
Bake . . . . at 350 degrees for 30 minutes or until cod tests done.

Marilou Lindall
Blair, Nebraska

 It's healthier to broil.

LOW-SODIUM RICE-STUFFED FLOUNDER

1 c. cooked rice
1/4 c. chopped cooked carrots
2 tbsp. chopped parsley
5 tbsp. melted butter
6 flounder fillets
1 1/2 tsp. flour
1/4 c. lemon juice
1 1/4 c. orange juice

Combine . . . . first 3 ingredients with 1 tablespoon melted butter in bowl, mixing well.
Spread . . . . . 1/4 cup mixture on each flounder fillet.
Roll . . . . fillets to enclose filling, fastening with toothpicks.
Place . . . . in shallow casserole.
Brush . . . . . . rolls with 2 tablespoons melted butter.
Bake . . . . at 350 degrees for 20 minutes or until fish flakes easily.
Stir . . . . flour into remaining butter in skillet, mixing well.
Add . . . . remaining ingredients, blending well.
Simmer . . . . . until thickened, stirring constantly.
Spoon . . . . . . over flounder rolls.
Garnish . . . . . with watercress.
Yields . . . . . . 6 servings.

Josie Henley
Akron, Ohio

MICROWAVE FLOUNDER ROSEMARY

1 sm. onion, thinly sliced
1 tbsp. butter
1 clove of garlic, minced
1/4 tsp. rosemary
1/8 tsp. pepper
1 can Cheddar cheese soup
1/2 c. drained chopped canned tomatoes
1 lb. fillets of flounder

Combine . . . . first 5 ingredients in glass saucepan, mixing well.
Microwave . . on High for 3 minutes or until onion is tender.
Add . . . . soup and tomatoes, blending well.
Arrange . . . . . flounder fillets in single layer in shallow glass dish.
Pour . . . . sauce over flounder.
Microwave . . on High for 15 minutes or until flounder flakes easily.
Yields . . . . . . 4 servings.

Kathy Bell
Bray, Connecticut

STEAMED FLOUNDER

2 tbsp. each soy sauce, Sherry
1 tbsp. oil
1 tsp. minced fresh gingerroot
1 lb. frozen flounder fillets, thawed, separated
3 lemon slices

Combine . . . . first 4 ingredients with 2 tablespoons water in wok.
Bring . . . . to a boil.
Arrange . . . . . flounder topped with lemon slices in wok.
Simmer . . . . . covered, for 10 minutes.
Arrange . . . . . on serving plate and spoon pan juices over flounder.
Garnish . . . . . with cucumber slices and chopped green onions.

Kay Banks
Crab Orchard, Tennessee

FOIL-BAKED HALIBUT

1 16-oz. package frozen halibut fillets, thawed
Salt and pepper

Paprika
4 tsp. lemon juice
2 carrots, cut into julienne strips
1 sm. green pepper, cut into rings
1 med. onion, sliced

Cut . . . . fish into 4 portions.
Place . . . . in centers of 4 pieces foil.
Sprinkle . . . . with salt, pepper, paprika and lemon juice.
Top . . . . with vegetables.
Fold . . . . foil, sealing edges.
Bake . . . . at 450 degrees for about 25 minutes or until fish flakes easily.
Yields . . . . . . 4 servings.

Anne Miller
Morganton, North Carolina

HALIBUT STEAK WITH ITALIAN SAUCE

1 lg. green pepper, cut into 1/2-in. strips
1 lg. onion, thinly sliced
1 1-lb. eggplant, peeled, cubed
2 8-oz. cans tomato sauce
1/2 c. dry white wine
1 clove of garlic, minced
1 bay leaf
2 tbsp. low-cholesterol margarine, melted
2 tbsp. lemon juice
Salt to taste
1/4 tsp. pepper
1 2-lb. halibut steak

Saute . . . . . . green pepper and onion in skillet until tender.
Add . . . . next 5 ingredients.
Simmer . . . . . for 15 minutes, stirring occasionally.
Combine . . . . next 4 ingredients in bowl, mixing well.
Place . . . . halibut steak on rack of broiler pan, brushing with lemon mixture.
Broil . . . . for 5 minutes.
Turn . . . . and baste again.
Broil . . . . for 5 minutes longer or until fish flakes easily.
Serve . . . . on warm platter surrounded by eggplant sauce.
Yields . . . . . . 6 servings.

Norma Tipton
Poulsbo, Washington

BAKED STUFFED SALMON

1 5 to 6-lb. salmon with backbone removed
1 tbsp. oil
1 tbsp. lemon juice
Dash of monosodium glutamate
1 med. onion, chopped
2 tbsp. butter
2 c. croutons
1 c. grated sharp cheese
1 c. chopped fresh parsley
1 sprig of dill
1/8 tsp. dry mustard
Salt and pepper to taste

Brush . . . . . . salmon with oil and lemon juice inside and out.
Sprinkle . . . . with monosodium glutamate.
Saute . . . . . . onion in butter in skillet until tender.
Stir . . . . in remaining ingredients, mixing well.
Stuff . . . . into salmon cavity; secure with string and wrap in heavy-duty foil.
Place . . . . in baking pan.
Bake . . . . at 375 degrees for 1 hour or until fish flakes easily.

Pattie Jacks
Oakland, Washington

SALMON QUICHE

1 unbaked 9-in. pastry shell
1 15 1/2-oz. can red salmon
3 lg. eggs, beaten
1 c. cottage cheese
2 tsp. Dijon mustard
3/4 tsp. salt
1/2 c. half and half
1 4-oz. can sliced mushrooms, drained
1/2 c. shredded carrots
1/4 c. sliced green onions

Prick . . . . bottom and side of pastry.
Bake . . . . at 375 degrees for 15 minutes.
Drain . . . . . . and flake salmon, reserving 2 tablespoons liquid.
Combine . . . . next 4 ingredients in large bowl, beating well.
Stir . . . . in remaining ingredients, re-served liquid and salmon.
Spoon . . . . . . into pastry shell.

Bake . . . . at 375 degrees for 45 minutes or until knife inserted in center comes out clean.
Let . . . . stand for 10 minutes before serving.
Yields . . . . . . 6-8 servings.

Lisa Richards
Harbor, Maine

GRILLED RED SNAPPER

1/2 c. butter, melted
1/4 c. lemon juice
3/4 tsp. Worcestershire sauce
1/4 tsp. onion salt
2 lb. red snapper

Mix . . . . first 4 ingredients in small bowl.
Grill . . . . snapper over hot coals for 5 to 8 minutes on each side, basting frequently.
Serve . . . . snapper with remaining sauce.
Yields . . . . . . 6-8 servings.

Earlene Jefferson
Mt. Ada, Florida

SAN FRANCISCO SOLE

2 lb. sole fillets
Salt
Dash of white pepper
1/2 c. chopped onion
2 tbsp. butter
1/4 c. dry white wine
1 8 3/4-oz. can seedless green grapes
3/4 c. half and half
1 egg yolk, beaten
1 tbsp. flour
Dash of nutmeg

Sprinkle . . . . sole fillets with salt and pepper.
Roll . . . . fillets, securing with toothpicks.
Saute . . . . . . onion in butter in skillet until tender.
Add . . . . fillets, wine and 1/4 cup grape liquid.
Simmer . . . . . covered, for 8 to 10 minutes or until fish flakes easily.
Place . . . . fillets on warm platter, removing picks; reserve liquid.
Combine . . . . remaining ingredients except grapes in bowl, blending well.

Add . . . . to hot liquid gradually.
Cook . . . . until thickened, stirring constantly.
Add . . . . drained grapes.
Pour . . . . over fillets, garnishing with paprika.
Broil . . . . about 5 inches from heat source for 5 minutes or until browned.
Yields . . . . . . 6 servings.

Dot Patrick
Zion, Illinois

SAUCY BAKED FILLETS

1 1/2 lb. haddock fillets
Salt and pepper to taste
Paprika
1 chicken bouillon cube
3 tbsp. flour
1 1/2 c. skim milk
1 tsp. Worcestershire sauce
1 1/2 tbsp. Sherry
1/2 tsp. rosemary
1/2 c. canned mushrooms

Place . . . . fish fillets in shallow casserole.
Sprinkle . . . . with salt, pepper and paprika.
Dissolve . . . . bouillon cube in 1/4 cup hot water in saucepan.
Blend . . . . . . in flour, mixing well.
Add . . . . milk, blending well.
Simmer . . . . . until sauce thickens, stirring constantly.
Stir . . . . in remaining ingredients.
Cook . . . . until heated through.
Pour . . . . over fish fillets.
Bake . . . . at 350 degrees for 25 minutes or until fish flakes easily.
Yields . . . . . . 6 servings.

Pearl V. Reed
Dallas, Texas

SPICY BROILED FISH

4 5-oz. turbot fish pieces
1 tbsp. lemon juice
1 pkg. Hidden Valley Ranch dressing mix

Place . . . . fish pieces on rack of broiler pan.
Sprinkle . . . . with remaining ingredients.
Broil . . . . for 6 minutes on each side.
Yields . . . . . . 4 servings.

Roberta Andrews
Cumberland, Tennessee

EASY TUNA SOUFFLE

1 7-oz. can tuna, flaked
1/2 tsp. salt
1/2 tsp. paprika
1 tsp. lemon juice
1 c. bread crumbs
3/4 c. milk
3 eggs, separated

Combine . . . . tuna with salt, paprika and lemon juice in bowl, mixing well.
Simmer . . . . . bread crumbs in milk in saucepan for 5 minutes.
Add . . . . milk mixture and beaten egg yolks to tuna mixture.
Fold . . . . stiffly beaten egg whites into tuna mixture.
Pour . . . . into greased baking dish.
Place . . . . in pan of hot water.
Bake . . . . at 350 degrees for 45 minutes or until set.
Serve . . . . immediately.
Yields . . . . . . 6 servings.

Linda Bass
Baldwin, North Carolina

FRIDAY NIGHT CASSEROLE

3 tbsp. butter
3 tbsp. flour
2 c. milk
1 tsp. mustard
1 tsp. horseradish sauce
2 c. leftover vegetables
1 can tuna
4 hard-boiled eggs, sliced

Melt . . . . butter in saucepan.
Blend . . . . . . in flour, stirring until smooth.
Stir . . . . in milk, blending well.
Simmer . . . . . until thickened, stirring constantly.
Add . . . . next 2 ingredients, blending well.
Place . . . . remaining ingredients in casserole, mixing well.
Pour . . . . white sauce over casserole.
Bake . . . . at 350 degrees for 20 minutes or until bubbly.
Yields . . . . . . 4 servings.

Dela Horn
Elkland, Wisconsin

MACARONI-TUNA BAKE

4 tbsp. butter
4 tbsp. flour
2 c. milk
1/2 tsp. salt
1 tsp. dry mustard
2 c. shredded cheese
2 c. macaroni, cooked, drained
1 can tuna, drained

Melt .... butter in saucepan.
Blend ...... in flour, stirring until smooth.
Stir .... in milk, blending well.
Simmer ..... until thickened, stirring constantly.
Add .... salt, mustard and cheese, blending well.
Stir .... in remaining ingredients, mixing well.
Pour .... into greased casserole.
Bake .... at 325 degrees for 30 minutes or until bubbly.
Yields ...... 4-6 servings.

Beulah Leoti
Duncan, Colorado

TUNA EXPRESS

3/4 c. mayonnaise
1 tbsp. lemon juice
1 tsp. Worcestershire sauce
1/2 tsp. dry mustard
1/4 tsp. Tabasco sauce
3 6 1/2-oz. cans tuna
1 c. finely chopped celery
1 c. finely cubed bread
1/2 c. chopped pecans
2 tbsp. minced onion
1/2 c. shredded Swiss cheese

Combine .... first 5 ingredients in bowl, blending well.
Add .... tuna, celery, bread, pecans and onion, tossing lightly.
Spoon ...... into shallow 1 1/2-quart casserole.
Bake .... at 350 degrees for 20 to 25 minutes or until bubbly.
Sprinkle .... cheese over top.
Bake .... for several minutes longer or until cheese melts.
Yields ...... 6 servings.

Photograph for this recipe on this page.

TUNA DIVAN

1 10-oz. package frozen broccoli
1 9 1/4-oz. can tuna
1/4 c. flour
1 tsp. salt
2 c. milk
1/3 c. grated Parmesan cheese
1 tbsp. lemon juice

Cook .... broccoli using package directions until tender-crisp; drain.
Drain ...... oil from tuna into saucepan.
Add .... flour and salt, stirring until smooth.
Stir .... in milk, blending well.
Simmer ..... until thickened, stirring constantly.
Add .... cheese and lemon juice, stirring until cheese melts.
Arrange ..... broccoli in casserole.
Spread ..... tuna over broccoli.
Cover ...... with cheese sauce.
Bake .... at 375 degrees for 20 minutes or until bubbly.
Yields ...... 6 servings.

Jessie Fayette
Fales, New Hampshire

TUNA-EGG CASSEROLE

2 7-oz. cans tuna, drained, flaked
2 tbsp. lemon juice
4 hard-boiled eggs, sliced
1 16-oz. can green peas
4 tbsp. butter
4 tbsp. flour
2 c. milk

1/2 tsp. salt
1/3 tsp. pepper
1 tsp. Worcestershire sauce
1 c. shredded cheese
1 c. fresh bread crumbs

Combine .... tuna with lemon juice in bowl, tossing to mix.
Layer ...... tuna mixture alternately with eggs and peas in casserole.
Melt .... butter in saucepan.
Blend ...... in flour, stirring until smooth.
Stir .... in milk, blending well.
Simmer .... until thickened, stirring constantly.
Add .... seasonings and cheese, stirring until cheese melts.
Pour .... over casserole.
Sprinkle .... bread crumbs over top.
Bake .... at 375 degrees for 1/2 hour or until bread crumbs are brown.
Yields ...... 8 servings.

Lee Mont
Oslo, Kansas

TUNA QUICHE

1 c. whole wheat flour
Sharp Cheddar cheese, shredded
1/4 c. chopped almonds
1/2 tsp. salt
1/4 tsp. paprika
6 tbsp. corn oil
2 cans water-pack tuna
3 eggs, beaten
1 c. sour cream
1/4 c. mayonnaise
1 tbsp. grated onion
1/4 tsp. dried dillweed
3 drops of hot pepper sauce

Combine .... flour, 2/3 cup cheese, almonds, salt and paprika in bowl, mixing well.
Stir .... in oil, blending well.
Reserve ..... 1/2 cup crust mixture.
Press .... remaining crust mixture over bottom and side of 9-inch pie plate.
Bake .... at 400 degrees for 10 minutes.
Drain ...... tuna, reserving liquid.
Add .... enough water to liquid to measure 1/2 cup.

Combine .... liquid with eggs, sour cream and mayonnaise in bowl, mixing well.
Add .... 1/2 cup cheese, tuna and remaining ingredients, blending well.
Spoon ...... into prepared crust.
Sprinkle .... with reserved crust mixture.
Bake .... at 325 degrees for 45 minutes or until center is set.
Yields ...... 6 servings.

Connie Tigue
Titus, Texas

FISHERMAN'S DELIGHT

1 sm. onion, chopped
1/4 c. margarine
1/4 c. flour
1 1/2 c. milk
1 tsp. parsley
Dash of pepper
1 sm. can mushrooms, drained
1 lb. whitefish, cut into cubes
1 sm. can shrimp, drained
3 potatoes, thinly sliced

Saute ...... onion in margarine in saucepan.
Stir .... in flour.
Add .... milk gradually, mixing well.
Cook .... until thick, stirring constantly.
Stir .... in parsley, pepper and mushrooms.
Arrange ..... whitefish and shrimp in buttered casserole.
Pour .... half the sauce over seafood.
Arrange ..... potatoes over sauce.
Top .... with remaining sauce.
Bake .... at 375 degrees for 1 hour or until potatoes are tender.

Coco Wilheim
Asheville, North Carolina

TOMATO-CLAM LUNCH

1 16-oz. can stewed tomatoes
1 6 1/2-oz. can minced clams
1 tsp. grated Romano cheese

Combine .... tomatoes and clams in saucepan.
Bring .... to a boil.
Sprinkle .... with cheese.
Yields ...... 2 servings.

Wendy Trask
Conners Corner, Iowa

CRAB DELIGHT

2 tbsp. chopped green pepper
2 tbsp. butter
2 tbsp. flour
Cayenne pepper to taste
1/2 tsp. mustard
1/4 tsp. salt
1/2 tsp. Worcestershire sauce
1 c. tomatoes
1 c. grated cheese
1 egg, slightly beaten
2/3 c. milk, scalded
1 c. flaked crab meat

Saute . . . . . . green pepper in butter in double boiler.
Stir . . . . in flour.
Add . . . . seasonings, tomatoes, cheese and egg, mixing well.
Cook . . . . over hot water for 10 minutes, stirring frequently.
Add . . . . milk gradually, stirring constantly.
Fold . . . . in crab meat.
Heat . . . . to serving temperature.
Serve . . . . over rice on toast.
Yields . . . . . . 6 servings.

Rene Newhart
Greenwich, Connecticut

CRAB JAMBALAYA

1 med. onion, chopped
1 clove of garlic, minced
2 tbsp. butter
1/2 chili pepper, chopped
1/8 tsp. white pepper
Dash of cayenne pepper
2 med. tomatoes, chopped
2 c. broth
2 c. crab meat
1 c. rice
Salt to taste

Saute . . . . . . onion and garlic in butter in skillet until brown.
Stir . . . . in remaining ingredients.
Simmer . . . . . covered, for 20 minutes.
Let . . . . stand until liquid is absorbed.
Yields . . . . . . 6 servings.

Allison Martin
Preston, California

DEVILED CRAB

3 hard-boiled eggs, separated
3 tbsp. butter, softened
2 tbsp. flour
2 1/2 c. milk
2 tbsp. chopped parsley
1 tsp. minced onion
2 c. flaked crab meat
Salt to taste
1/4 tsp. paprika
2 tbsp. Worcestershire sauce (opt.)
1/3 c. bread crumbs

Mash . . . . egg yolks with 1 1/2 tablespoons butter in bowl.
Melt . . . . remaining 1 1/2 tablespoons butter in saucepan.
Blend . . . . . . in flour.
Add . . . . egg yolks, mixing well.
Stir . . . . in milk gradually.
Cook . . . . until thick, stirring constantly.
Add . . . . chopped egg whites with next 6 ingredients, mixing well.
Pour . . . . into greased casserole.
Top . . . . with crumbs.
Bake . . . . at 350 degrees for 10 minutes.

Jo Anne White
Anniston, Alabama

KING CRAB PARMESAN

1 med. onion, chopped
2 tbsp. butter
4 tbsp. flour
2 c. skim milk
MSG, thyme, seasoned salt and pepper to taste
4 c. King crab
Corn flake crumbs
Parmesan cheese

Saute . . . . . . onion in butter in skillet until brown.
Blend . . . . . . in flour.
Stir . . . . in milk gradually.
Cook . . . . until thick, stirring constantly.
Stir . . . . in seasonings.
Layer . . . . . . crab and corn flake crumbs in baking dish.
Spoon . . . . . . sauce over layers.
Sprinkle . . . . with cheese.
Bake . . . . at 350 degrees for 30 minutes.

Jana Rawlins
Ansonia, Michigan

SOUTH AFRICAN ROCK LOBSTER CASSEROLE

*24 oz. frozen South African rock
    lobster tails
Salt to taste
1 lb. mushrooms, sliced
1 c. onion, chopped
1 bay leaf
1 tsp. dried tarragon
2 tbsp. cornstarch
2 c. low-fat yogurt
4 oz. water chestnuts, sliced
Pepper to taste*

Drop . . . . rock lobster tails into boiling salted water in saucepan.
Cook . . . . for 2 minutes after water returns to a boil.
Drain . . . . . . and rinse with cold water.
Cut . . . . away underside membrane, removing and slicing meat; set aside.
Combine . . . . mushrooms, onion, bay leaf and tarragon in 1/4 cup water in small saucepan.
Simmer . . . . . until mushrooms are tender.
Remove . . . . bay leaf.
Mix . . . . cornstarch with a small amount of water to make a paste.
Combine . . . . cornstarch paste and yogurt in large saucepan.
Simmer . . . . . until thickened, stirring constantly.
Add . . . . vegetables, rock lobster slices, water chestnuts and seasonings, mixing lightly.
Pour . . . . into casserole.
Bake . . . . at 350 degrees for 20 minutes.
Yields . . . . . . 6 servings.

Photograph for this recipe on page 4.

 Eat balanced meals each day, being sure to cover the four basic food groups adequately.

LOBSTER FRITTO AND FONDUE

*2 lb. frozen lobster tails
Sliced zucchini, mushrooms, green peppers*

*Cauliflowerets
1 c. butter
3 c. oil
1 tsp. aromatic bitters
Salt and pepper to taste
1 lb. Swiss cheese, grated
3 tbsp. flour
2 c. dry white wine
3 tbsp. Brandy*

Place . . . . lobster tails in boiling salted water in saucepan.
Boil . . . . for 2 to 3 minutes; do not overcook.
Remove . . . . lobster from shells, chopping into bite-sized pieces.
Arrange . . . . . lobster in center of serving dish surrounded by vegetables.
Chill . . . . in refrigerator.
Combine . . . . butter, oil, bitters, salt and pepper in chafing dish over flame.
Mix . . . . cheese and flour in bowl.
Heat . . . . wine in fondue pot over flame.
Add . . . . cheese gradually, mixing well after each addition.
Stir . . . . in Brandy.
Cook . . . . vegetables and heat lobster on fondue forks in oil mixture.
Dip . . . . into fondue.

Photograph for this recipe on this page.

OYSTERS CASINO

3 slices bacon, chopped
4 tbsp. chopped onion
2 tbsp. each chopped green pepper,
  celery
1/2 tsp. each salt, pepper
1/2 tsp. Worcestershire sauce
2 drops of hot sauce
1 tsp. lemon juice
1 pt. oysters, drained

Saute ...... first 4 ingredients in skillet.
Stir .... in remaining ingredients except oysters.
Arrange ..... oysters in buttered baking dish.
Top .... with sauce.
Bake .... at 350 degrees for 20 minutes or until brown.
Yields ...... 4 servings.

Regina Smith
Yakushka Bay, Oregon

EGGPLANT-OYSTER CASSEROLE

2 med. eggplant
2 10-oz. cans oysters
3/4 c. butter
1/2 lb. fresh mushrooms, sliced
1/4 c. chopped shallots
1 c. seasoned bread crumbs
1/4 to 1/2 tsp. Tabasco sauce
1/4 c. chopped parsley
3 cloves of garlic, minced
1 tsp. basil
1/2 tsp. thyme
Salt to taste
1 c. grated Cheddar cheese
1/2 c. evaporated milk

Wash .... eggplant and prick with fork.
Bake .... at 350 degrees for 1/2 hour or until very tender; cool.
Peel .... and cut into 1/4-inch slices.
Cook .... oysters in oyster liquid in saucepan until edges curl.
Remove .... oysters, chopping finely.
Add .... 1/4 cup butter, mushrooms and 2 tablespoons shallots to saucepan.
Simmer ..... for 10 minutes.
Add .... oysters, 1/2 cup crumbs and Tabasco sauce, mixing well; set aside.

Saute ...... remaining shallots in 1/4 cup butter in skillet for 5 minutes.
Add .... parsley, garlic, basil, thyme, salt and remaining 1/2 cup crumbs, mixing well.
Layer ...... half the eggplant, crumb and oyster mixtures in 6 x 10-inch shallow baking dish.
Repeat ..... layers with remaining ingredients.
Sprinkle .... cheese over top.
Drizzle ..... with evaporated milk.
Dot .... with remaining 1/4 cup butter.
Bake .... at 350 degrees for 1/2 hour.
Yields ...... 4-6 servings.

Photograph for this recipe on page 51.

MICROWAVE SCALLOPS WITH VEGETABLES

12 oz. frozen scallops
1/4 lb. fresh mushrooms, sliced
1 sm. onion, sliced
1/2 green pepper, sliced
Salt and pepper to taste

Microwave .. scallops in covered casserole on High for 3 minutes.
Add .... vegetables.
Microwave .. on High for 8 to 10 minutes.
Season ..... with salt and pepper.
Yields ...... 2 servings.

Gillian Edwards
Cairo, Illinois

SEAFOOD MEDLEY

2 tbsp. chopped shallots
1 c. chopped mushrooms
Butter
1 tsp. dry mustard
1/2 tsp. chopped tarragon leaves
1 c. chopped cooked shrimp
1 c. cooked scallops
1 c. chopped cooked lobster
1 c. cream
1 tbsp. cornstarch
Salt and pepper to taste

Saute ...... shallots and mushrooms in a small amount of butter in skillet for 5 minutes.
Stir .... in next 6 ingredients.
Bring .... to a boil.

Blend ......cornstarch with a small amount of water.
Stir ....into mixture.
Cook ....until thick, stirring constantly and season to taste.
Yields ......4 servings.

Polly Price
Barstow, California

SHRIMP A LA POPPY

1 onion, chopped
1 green pepper, chopped
1 tbsp. oil
2 tomatoes, chopped
1/3 c. dry white wine
1 tbsp. chopped fresh basil
Salt and pepper to taste
1/4 lb. shelled shrimp

Saute ......onion and green pepper in oil in skillet until tender.
Add ....remaining ingredients except shrimp.
Simmer .....for 15 minutes.
Add ....shrimp.
Cook ....for 5 minutes longer.
Serve ....immediately with sprinkle of fresh chopped parsley.

Poppy Sampson
Erie, Pennsylvania

SHRIMP-CRAB CASSEROLE

1 sm. can crab meat, drained
1 1/2 lb. boiled shrimp, cleaned
1/2 green pepper, chopped (opt.)
1/2 c. chopped onion
1 sm. jar pimentos, drained, chopped
1 c. chopped celery
1 tbsp. Worcestershire sauce
1 sm. can mushrooms, drained, chopped
1 c. mayonnaise
3/4 c. evaporated milk
1 c. rice, cooked
Salt and pepper to taste

Combine ....all ingredients in bowl, mixing well.
Spoon ......into 11 x 14-inch baking dish.
Bake ....at 350 degrees for 1/2 hour.
Yields ......10 servings.

Nadine Price
Chicago, Illinois

SHRIMP IN GARLIC SAUCE

2 lb. shrimp
2 tbsp. oil
2 sm. cloves of garlic, minced
1 6-oz. can tomato paste
2 tsp. salt
1/2 tsp. each pepper, basil
1/2 c. chopped onion

Saute ......shrimp in oil in skillet for 5 minutes or until pink.
Add ....remaining ingredients with 1 cup water, mixing well.
Simmer .....until heated through.
Yields ......6 servings.

Jobeth Bellows
Joplin, Missouri

FAVORITE SHRIMP CURRY

4 c. sliced mushrooms
1 c. finely chopped onions
2 cloves of garlic, crushed
4 med. tomatoes, peeled, chopped
1 tbsp. curry powder
1 tsp. chili powder
Salt and pepper to taste
2 lb. shrimp, peeled
2 tbsp. cornstarch
1 c. yogurt
2 c. cooked rice

Saute ......first 3 ingredients in large skillet for 3 to 5 minutes or until tender.
Stir ....in tomatoes and seasonings.
Simmer .....for 10 to 12 minutes, stirring occasionally.
Add ....shrimp.
Cook ....covered, for 7 to 10 minutes or until shrimp are pink.
Dissolve ....cornstarch in 1 tablespoon water in small bowl.
Stir ....into shrimp mixture.
Cook ....until thick, stirring constantly; remove from heat.
Add ....yogurt, mixing well.
Heat ....just to serving temperature; do not boil.
Serve ....with rice.

Kathi Foged
Papillion, Nebraska

SHRIMP CREOLE DELUXE

2 med. onions, finely chopped
2 green peppers, finely chopped
4 stalks celery, finely chopped
1 clove of garlic, minced
3 tbsp. oil
1 8-oz. can tomato sauce
1 tsp. chili powder
1/2 tsp. hot sauce
1 tbsp. Worcestershire sauce
Salt to taste
1/2 tsp. pepper
1 to 1 1/2 lb. shrimp, shelled

Saute ...... first 4 ingredients in oil in skillet until tender.
Stir .... in remaining ingredients except shrimp.
Simmer ..... for 30 minutes.
Add .... shrimp.
Cook .... covered, for 30 to 40 minutes.
Serve .... over rice.
Yields ...... 4-5 servings.

Millie Rutherford
Milford, Nebraska

MICROWAVE SHRIMP JAMBALAYA

3 tbsp. oil
3 tbsp. flour
2 c. finely chopped onion
1/2 c. finely chopped green pepper
4 cloves of garlic, finely chopped
1 10-oz. can chopped tomatoes
2 c. shrimp, peeled
2 c. diced ham
3 c. cooked rice
1 tbsp. each chopped parsley, chopped green onion tops

Mix .... oil and flour in 3-quart glass casserole.
Microwave .. on High for 5 to 6 minutes or until lightly browned.
Add .... onion, green pepper and garlic, mixing well.
Microwave .. on High for 3 minutes.
Add .... tomatoes, shrimp and 1 1/2 cups hot water, mixing well.
Microwave .. on High for 7 minutes or until shrimp are pink.
Stir .... in ham and rice.

Microwave .. covered, on High for 3 minutes.
Sprinkle .... parsley and onion tops over casserole.
Yields ...... 6 servings.

Kitty Cardwell
St. Louis, Missouri

ORIENTAL SHRIMP AND RICE CASSEROLE

1 lb. peeled shrimp
2 tbsp. butter
2 c. each chopped celery, onion
6 stalks bok choy, chopped
1 pkg. frozen Chinese vegetables
1 1/2 c. chicken broth
1/4 c. soy sauce
2 tbsp. cornstarch
2 to 3 c. cooked rice

Saute ...... shrimp in butter in skillet until pink.
Add .... next 3 ingredients.
Cook .... for 3 minutes.
Stir .... in Chinese vegetables.
Simmer ..... covered, for several minutes.
Combine .... broth, soy sauce and cornstarch in small bowl.
Pour .... over vegetable mixture.
Cook .... until thick, stirring constantly.
Place .... rice in casserole.
Pour .... shrimp mixture over top.
Bake .... at 350 degrees for 1/2 hour.

Vesta Deal
White Plains, New York

SHRIMP EGG FOO YUNG

2 c. fresh bean sprouts
6 eggs, beaten
3 scallions, finely chopped
1 c. cooked shrimp, chopped

Combine .... all ingredients in bowl, mixing well.
Pour .... 1/2 cup at a time into small hot oiled skillet.
Brown ...... on both sides.
Serve .... with soy sauce.
Yields ...... 6 servings.

Jodie Harrow
Blankston, Texas

poultry

CHICKEN IMPERIAL

3 chicken breasts, halved, boned
Salt and pepper to taste
1/4 c. margarine
2 tbsp. Worcestershire sauce
1 tsp. each curry powder, oregano
1/2 tsp. each dry mustard, garlic powder
1/4 tsp. paprika
Tabasco sauce to taste
1/3 c. dry Sherry

Sprinkle .... chicken with salt and pepper.
Place .... in large shallow casserole.
Combine .... remaining ingredients in saucepan.
Cook .... over medium heat until well blended.
Pour .... over chicken.
Bake .... covered, at 350 degrees for 1 to 1 1/2 hours or until chicken is tender, turning chicken several times during baking.
Yields ...... 4-6 servings.

May Chaplain
Londonderry, New Hampshire

MEAL-IN-ONE BAKE

3 chicken bouillon cubes
3 cooked chicken breasts, chopped
1 10-oz. package frozen broccoli, thawed
1 c. coarsely shredded cabbage
1/2 c. shredded carrots
1/4 sm. red onion, finely chopped
1/2 c. skim milk

Dissolve .... bouillon cubes in 1/4 cup hot water.
Combine .... with remaining ingredients in bowl, mixing well.
Spoon ...... into lightly greased casserole.
Bake .... covered, at 325 degrees for 30 minutes.
Yields ...... 4-6 servings.

Jamie Christian
Blytheville, Arkansas

SESAME CHICKEN

4 10-oz. chicken breasts, skinned
1/4 c. soy sauce
1/4 c. lemon juice

4 tsp. artificial sweetener
4 tsp. sesame seed
1 tsp. dillweed
1/4 tsp. garlic powder
Pepper to taste
2 tbsp. dry onion flakes

Place .... chicken in shallow baking dish.
Mix .... next 3 ingredients in bowl.
Pour .... over chicken.
Sprinkle .... sesame seed and remaining ingredients over top.
Chill .... overnight.
Bake .... at 350 degrees for 1 1/2 hours.
Yields ...... 4 servings.

Charleen Janus
Evansville, Wisconsin

ALMOND-CHICKEN WITH RICE

1 lb. chicken breasts, boned, skinned
1 tsp. garlic salt
1 1-lb. can fancy Chinese vegetables
1 c. thinly sliced celery
1 tbsp. cornstarch
1 tsp. sugar
2 tbsp. soy sauce
1/3 c. chicken broth
1/2 c. blanched almonds
1 c. well-drained pineapple tidbits
3 c. hot cooked rice
1/3 c. thinly sliced green onions

Cut .... chicken into thin strips.
Sprinkle .... with garlic salt.
Saute ...... in skillet until browned.
Drain ...... Chinese vegetables, reserving liquid.
Add .... Chinese vegetables, celery and 1/3 cup reserved liquid to chicken.
Steam ...... covered, for 3 minutes.
Mix .... next 4 ingredients in bowl.
Stir .... into chicken mixture with half the almonds.
Cook .... until thick, stirring constantly.
Add .... pineapple.
Serve .... over rice.
Top .... with onions and remaining almonds.
Yields ...... 6 servings.

Beverlee Brown Williams
Campbell, California

SLIM BROCCOLI-CHICKEN

2 lg. chicken breasts, skinned, boned, cubed
Salt and pepper to taste
1/4 c. chopped onion
2 tbsp. margarine
1   10-oz. package frozen chopped
     broccoli, thawed
1 tsp. lemon juice
1/4 tsp. thyme
3 med. tomatoes, cut into wedges

Sprinkle .... chicken with salt and pepper.
Saute ...... with onion in margarine in skillet.
Stir .... in broccoli, lemon juice, thyme and salt and pepper to taste.
Simmer ..... covered, for 6 minutes.
Add .... tomatoes.
Simmer ..... covered, for 4 minutes longer.
Yields ...... 4 servings.

Leola R. Becker
Hustisford, Wisconsin

CHICKEN BREASTS AND MUSHROOMS

3 chicken breasts, halved, boned
2 tbsp. lemon juice
Salt and white pepper to taste
1/2 lb. fresh mushrooms, sliced
1/2 c. finely chopped onion
3 tbsp. margarine
1/3 c. flour
2 tbsp. oil
1/2 c. dry white wine
1 bay leaf
1/2 tsp. tarragon, crumbled

Season ..... chicken with lemon juice, salt and pepper; set aside.
Saute ...... mushrooms and onion in margarine in skillet for 5 minutes; remove.
Coat .... chicken with flour.
Brown ...... in oil added to pan drippings for 10 to 15 minutes.
Stir .... in sauteed vegetables and remaining ingredients.
Simmer ..... until chicken is tender.
Yields ...... 6 servings.

Marian Danner
Croft Corners, New Hampshire

MOO GOO GAI PAN

2 whole chicken breasts, boned, cubed
1/2 tsp. salt
1 tsp. cornstarch
2 tbsp. peanut oil
1 c. diagonally sliced celery
1   4-oz. can mushrooms
1 green pepper, chopped
1   5-oz. can sliced water chestnuts,
     drained
1 tbsp. soy sauce
1/4 c. slivered almonds

Sprinkle .... chicken with salt and cornstarch.
Stir-fry ..... in hot oil in skillet for 2 minutes.
Add .... celery.
Cook .... for 2 minutes.
Stir .... in remaining ingredients except almonds.
Cook .... for 4 minutes longer.
Add .... almonds, mixing well.
Yields ...... 4 servings.

Marilyn Musgrave
Robinson, Illinois

ORIENTAL CHICKEN

4 chicken breasts, skinned, boned, slivered
1 pkg. frozen French-style green beans
1 can Chinese vegetables
3 tbsp. cider vinegar
1/4 tsp. pepper
2 tbsp. cornstarch
3 tbsp. soy sauce
3 med. tomatoes, cut in 6 wedges

Saute ...... chicken in skillet for 10 minutes; push to side of skillet.
Saute ...... green beans for 5 minutes.
Stir .... in Chinese vegetables, vinegar, and pepper.
Simmer ..... covered, for 5 minutes.
Blend ...... cornstarch with 2 tablespoons water.
Stir .... into skillet with soy sauce.
Cook .... until thick, stirring constantly.
Arrange ..... tomatoes over top.
Cook .... for several minutes longer.
Serve .... over rice.

Kay Apple
Abilene, Texas

STIR-FRY CHICKEN

3 chicken breasts, cooked, cut into
   2-in. strips
1 tbsp. soy sauce
1/4 c. chopped onion
2 sm. cloves of garlic, minced
1/2 green pepper, cut in strips
1 c. diagonally sliced celery
1 c. frozen snow peas
1 c. drained bean sprouts
1/2 c. sliced drained mushrooms
1/4 c. bamboo shoots
2 pkg. instant chicken broth

Combine . . . . first 4 ingredients with 1 cup water in large nonstick skillet.
Cook . . . . until tender, stirring occasionally.
Add . . . . green pepper, celery and snow peas.
Cook . . . . . . for 3 to 5 minutes or until tender-crisp.
Stir . . . . in remaining ingredients.
Heat . . . . to serving temperature.
Serve . . . . over rice.
Yields . . . . . . 3 servings.

Kathy Overholt
Johnson City, Tennessee

SWEET AND SOUR CHICKEN

6 chicken breasts, boned, slivered
2 cloves of garlic, crushed
1/3 c. oil
1   8-oz. can pineapple chunks
1   4-oz. jar sweet mixed pickles
2 tsp. soy sauce
1/2 c. slivered green pepper

Saute . . . . . . chicken with garlic in oil in skillet over high heat for 2 minutes.
Drain . . . . . . pineapple and pickles, reserving juices.
Add . . . . reserved juices and soy sauce to skillet, mixing well.
Simmer . . . . . until chicken is tender.
Stir . . . . in pineapple, pickles and green pepper.
Heat . . . . to serving temperature.
Serve . . . . over rice.
Garnish . . . . . with tomato wedges.

Lonnie Quesenberry
Granston, Montana

SWEET AND SOUR CHICKEN STIR FRY

1/2 c. low-sugar apricot spread
1 tbsp. vinegar
1 tsp. each garlic salt, ginger
1 tsp. soy sauce
1/8 tsp. crushed red pepper
2 med. zucchini, halved, sliced
1/2 lb. small mushrooms
1/4 c. oil
1/2 tsp. salt
2 lg. chicken breasts, skinned, boned, cubed
1   6-oz. package frozen pea pods, thawed

Combine . . . . first 6 ingredients in bowl, mixing well.
Stir-fry . . . . . zucchini and mushrooms in 2 tablespoons oil in skillet until tender-crisp; add salt.
Place . . . . on heated platter.
Stir-fry . . . . . chicken in remaining oil until tender.
Stir . . . . in zucchini mixture and pea pods.
Pour . . . . in apricot sauce tossing gently to mix and heat to serving temperature.
Serve . . . . with rice.
Yields . . . . . . 4 servings.

Photograph for this recipe above.

CHICKEN NUGGETS

4 chicken breasts, skinned, boned
1/2 c. margarine, melted
1/2 c. dry bread crumbs
1/4 c. Parmesan cheese
1 tsp. each salt, thyme, basil

Cut .... each chicken breast into 12 pieces.
Dip .... each piece in margarine.
Coat .... with mixture of remaining ingredients.
Place .... on baking sheet.
Bake .... at 400 degrees for 10 to 15 minutes or until brown.

Joan Cahill
Little Rock, Arkansas

BAKED CHICKEN WITH PECANS

1 c. flour
1 c. chopped pecans
1/4 c. sesame seed
3/4 tsp. salt
1 tbsp. paprika
1/2 tsp. pepper
1 c. buttermilk
1 egg, slightly beaten
1/2 c. butter
1 frying chicken, cut up

Combine .... first 6 ingredients in bowl, mixing well.
Combine .... buttermilk and egg in bowl, mixing well.
Melt .... butter in casserole.
Dip .... chicken in milk mixture.
Coat .... with pecan mixture.
Place .... in melted butter, turning to coat both sides.
Bake .... at 350 degrees for 1 1/2 hours or until brown and tender, basting several times.

Wanda Nada
Washington, D. C.

CHICKEN CACCIATORE

1 2 to 3-lb. frying chicken, cut up
1 clove of garlic, sliced
1/2 c. olive oil
1 sm. can tomatoes, drained
1 1/4 tsp. salt

1 tsp. rosemary
1 tsp. chopped parsley
1 tsp. pepper
1 sm. can mushrooms, drained
1 c. white cooking wine
1 sm. jar green olives, drained, chopped

Brown ...... chicken with garlic in hot oil in Dutch oven; drain.
Add .... remaining ingredients.
Simmer ..... 15 minutes.
Bake .... at 375 degrees for 1/2 hour or until chicken is tender.
Serve .... over rice.
Yields ...... 4 servings.

Jeanette Jones
Bristol, Tennessee

CRISPY CHICKEN

1 2-lb. fryer, cut up
3/4 c. crushed Grape Nuts
2 tsp. garlic salt
1/8 tsp. pepper
2 tbsp. oil

Coat .... chicken with mixture of Grape Nuts, garlic salt and pepper.
Place .... in baking pan.
Sprinkle .... with oil.
Bake .... at 400 degrees for 50 minutes or until brown and tender.

Mrs. Beverly J. Keck
Palmyra, Missouri

FRENCH-BAKED CHICKEN

1 fryer, cut up
1 tsp. salt
1 tsp. pepper
1 tsp. onion salt
1/3 c. low-calorie French dressing

Season ..... chicken with next 3 ingredients.
Place .... in single layer in shallow baking pan.
Baste .... with French dressing.
Bake .... covered, at 350 degrees for 1/2 hour.
Baste .... with French dressing.
Bake .... uncovered, 15 minutes longer or until brown and tender.
Yields ...... 4-5 servings.

Mrs. Mary C. Fuller
Montgomery, Alabama

CHICKEN CURRY SUPREME

2 c. sliced mushrooms
1/2 c. diced onion
3 tbsp. butter
3 tbsp. flour
1 1/2 tsp. curry powder
Salt and pepper to taste
3/4 c. milk
1 c. chicken broth
3 c. cooked cubed chicken

Saute ...... mushrooms and onion in butter in skillet.
Stir .... in flour and seasonings until well mixed.
Add .... milk and chicken broth gradually.
Simmer .... until thickened, stirring constantly.
Stir .... in chicken.
Spoon ...... into casserole.
Bake .... at 350 degrees for 30 minutes or until bubbly.
Serve .... over rice or noodles.

Martha Steiger
Lima, Ohio

PEACHY BAKED CHICKEN

3 chicken thighs
3 chicken breasts, halved
3 chicken drumsticks
1 16-oz. can peach halves in light syrup
2 tbsp. orange juice
1 tbsp. soy sauce
Dash of ginger
Pepper to taste

Place .... chicken in single layer in baking dish.
Drain ...... peaches, reserving syrup.
Mix .... reserved syrup with remaining ingredients except peach halves in bowl.
Bake .... chicken at 400 degrees for 1 hour or until tender, basting with syrup mixture every 15 minutes.
Add .... peach halves to chicken.
Baste .... with syrup mixture.
Bake .... 5 minutes longer.
Yields ...... 6 servings.

Diane M. Intoccio
Marietta, Ohio

CHICKEN OREGANO

1 tsp. oregano
1/2 tsp. salt
1/4 tsp. pepper
1 clove of garlic or 1/2 tsp. garlic salt
Juice of 2 lemons
1 2 1/2-lb. fryer
1/2 stick margarine, melted

Combine .... first 5 ingredients, mixing well.
Rub .... chicken cavity and cut side with juice mixture.
Place .... in 7 x 10-inch pan.
Brush ...... with margarine.
Pour .... in 1 cup water.
Bake .... at 400 degrees until golden brown.
Lower ...... temperature to 350 degrees.
Bake .... 30 minutes longer or until tender, basting frequently.

Kathy Benson
Marion, South Carolina

CHICKEN PICCATA

1 tsp. salt
1/2 tsp. pepper
2 tsp. poultry seasoning
2 tsp. dried basil
2 tsp. rosemary
2 chickens, halved

Combine .... first 5 ingredients in bowl, mixing well.
Arrange ..... chicken, skin side down, in single layer in shallow baking dish.
Sprinkle .... half the mixture over chicken.
Bake .... covered, at 425 degrees for 1/2 hour.
Turn .... chicken and sprinkle with remaining mixture.
Bake .... uncovered, 1/2 hour longer or until brown and tender.

Laurel Hill
Canver, Maryland

CHICKEN PUFF

1 1/2 c. flour
2 tsp. baking powder
Salt to taste
2 eggs, separated

1 c. milk
2 c. cooked chopped chicken
2 tsp. grated onion
1/4 to 1/2 c. grated carrot
2 tbsp. melted butter
1 1/2 c. chicken gravy

Mix . . . . first 3 ingredients in bowl.
Stir . . . . in beaten egg yolks and milk.
Add . . . . chicken, onion, carrot and butter, mixing well.
Fold . . . . in stiffly beaten egg whites.
Place . . . . in greased baking dish.
Bake . . . . at 425 degrees for 25 minutes or until lightly browned.
Serve . . . . with hot chicken gravy.
Yields . . . . . . 6 servings.

Jackie Mayne
Ardmore, North Carolina

CHICKEN AND BROCCOLI CASSEROLE

1/4 c. chopped onions
2 tbsp. butter
1/4 c. flour
1 lg. can evaporated skim milk
Salt and pepper to taste
1/2 tsp. curry powder
1 4-oz. can sliced mushrooms
1 10-oz. package broccoli spears, cooked, drained
1 chicken, cooked, diced
1 c. shredded Monterey Jack cheese

Saute . . . . . . onions in butter in skillet until tender.
Blend . . . . . . in flour.
Add . . . . evaporated skim milk, stirring to mix well.
Simmer . . . . . until thickened, stirring constantly.
Stir . . . . in seasonings and mushrooms.
Arrange . . . . . broccoli and chicken in casserole.
Pour . . . . sauce over casserole.
Top . . . . with cheese.
Bake . . . . at 375 degrees for 20 minutes or until bubbly.
Let . . . . stand for 15 minutes before serving.
Yields . . . . . . 6 servings.

Sylvia Conte
Scranton, Pennsylvania

CHICKEN AND BROCCOLI SUPREME

1/3 box buttery crackers, crushed
2 boxes frozen chopped broccoli, cooked, drained
4 c. chicken, cooked, chopped
1/4 lb. Velveeta cheese, cubed
1 sm. can mushrooms
2 c. chicken broth

Place . . . . half the cracker crumbs in greased casserole.
Add . . . . broccoli and chicken.
Heat . . . . remaining ingredients in saucepan until cheese melts, stirring constantly.
Pour . . . . over casserole.
Top . . . . with remaining cracker crumbs.
Bake . . . . at 350 degrees for 30 minutes or until bubbly.

Linda Harris
Lima, Ohio

BAKED CHICKEN CASSEROLE

2 c. skim milk
1/4 c. flour
2 chicken bouillon cubes
2 c. diced cooked chicken
1/2 tsp. marjoram
Salt and pepper to taste
1/4 c. chopped parsley
1/4 c. chopped onion
1 c. diced celery
3 to 5 fresh mushrooms, sliced
2 tbsp. chopped green pepper
1 c. elbow macaroni, cooked

Combine . . . . milk and flour in saucepan, blending well.
Add . . . . bouillon cubes, stirring to dissolve.
Simmer . . . . . until thickened, stirring constantly.
Add . . . . remaining ingredients, mixing well.
Spoon . . . . . . into casserole.
Bake . . . . at 350 degrees for 25 minutes or until bubbly.
Yields . . . . . . 5 servings.

Sherry Zeigler
Chillicothe, Ohio

CHICKEN DELUXE

1 frying chicken, cut up
3 sm. zucchini, sliced
1 sm. onion, diced
2 tbsp. tomato sauce
Paprika to taste
Salt and pepper to taste
Garlic powder to taste
Crushed red pepper to taste
Minced parsley to taste
1 pkg. frozen spatzels, cooked, drained
1/4 c. grated Romano cheese

Saute ...... chicken in skillet until brown.
Cook .... covered, over low heat for 15 minutes or until tender.
Remove .... and place in casserole.
Saute ...... zucchini and onion in skillet for 5 minutes.
Add .... tomato sauce and seasonings with 1/2 cup water.
Layer ...... spatzels over chicken.
Top .... with tomato sauce mixture.
Sprinkle .... with cheese.
Bake .... at 325 degrees for 10 minutes or until serving temperature.

Mrs. Florence Calderone
Youngstown, Ohio

COMPANY CHICKEN EXOTICA

1 3-lb. frying chicken, cut up
1/2 c. olive oil
2 c. instant rice
2 c. chopped onions
1 clove of garlic, minced
1 1-lb. can whole tomatoes
1 can chicken broth
1 4-oz. can chopped green chili peppers
1/2 tsp. saffron
1/2 tsp. crushed red pepper
Salt to taste
1/2 tsp. pepper
1/2 pkg. frozen green peas
1 c. pimento-stuffed olives

Brown ...... chicken in hot oil in Dutch oven; remove chicken.
Add .... rice, onions and garlic.
Brown ...... lightly, stirring occasionally.
Add .... chicken and next 7 ingredients.
Bring .... to a boil.

Bake .... covered, at 325 degrees for 1 hour or until chicken is tender.
Stir .... in 1 cup water.
Sprinkle .... frozen peas and olives over top.
Bake .... 20 minutes longer.
Yields ...... 6 servings.

Loretha Roper
Canute, Oklahoma

CHICKEN LASAGNA

2/3 c. milk
Salt to taste
1/2 tsp. poultry seasoning
2 3-oz. packages cream cheese, softened
1 c. cream-style cottage cheese
1/3 c. sliced stuffed green olives
1/3 c. minced onion
1/3 c. minced green pepper
1/4 c. minced parsley
3 c. diced cooked chicken
8 oz. wide or lasagna noodles, cooked
1/2 c. bread crumbs

Combine .... first 10 ingredients in large bowl, mixing well.
Layer ...... noodles and chicken mixture alternately into 11 1/2 x 7 1/2-inch casserole.
Top .... with crumbs.
Bake .... at 375 degrees for 30 minutes or until bubbly.
Let .... stand 10 minutes before serving.
Yields ...... 8 servings.

Angie Carman
Rapid City, South Dakota

SUPERB CHICKEN SPAGHETTI

1 4 to 5-lb. chicken
1 8-oz. package spaghetti
1 green pepper, chopped
1 clove of garlic, minced
1 lg. onion, chopped
Salt to taste
1 sm. can pimento, chopped
1 8-oz. can tomato juice
Grated cheese

Cook .... chicken in saucepan with water to cover until tender.
Remove .... chicken, reserving broth.
Debone ..... and chop chicken.

Cook . . . . spaghetti in reserved broth until tender; drain.

Saute . . . . . . pepper, garlic and onion in skillet until tender.

Combine . . . . chicken, spaghetti, vegetables and next 3 ingredients in casserole, mixing well.

Bake . . . . at 350 degrees for 1 hour.

Sprinkle . . . . with cheese.

Bake . . . . until cheese melts.

Nancy Salines
Akron, Ohio

SIMPLE CHICKEN TETRAZZINI

2 tbsp. butter
2 tbsp. flour
Salt and pepper to taste
1/2 c. chicken broth
1 c. milk
2 c. diced cooked chicken
1 sm. jar pimentos, chopped (opt.)
4 oz. spaghetti, cooked
1/4 c. grated sharp cheese

Melt . . . . butter in saucepan.

Stir . . . . in flour and seasonings until smooth.

Add . . . . broth and milk gradually, blending well.

Simmer . . . . . until thickened, stirring constantly.

Stir . . . . in chicken, pimentos and spaghetti.

Spoon . . . . . . into 2-quart casserole.

Sprinkle . . . . with cheese.

Bake . . . . at 375 degrees for 15 minutes or until lightly browned.

Jerri Ashmore
Louisville, Kentucky

CHICKEN WITH VEGETABLES

Salt and pepper to taste
2 sm. eggplant, peeled, chopped
3/4 lb. cut green beans
1/4 lb. okra, sliced 1/2-in. thick
2 sm. onions, sliced
4 green peppers, finely chopped
2 chickens, cut up
2 lg. tomatoes, sliced
2 1/2 c. chicken broth, heated

Salt . . . . eggplant; let stand for 1/2 hour.

Layer . . . . . . green beans, okra, onions and peppers in large casserole.

Rinse . . . . . . and drain eggplant.

Place . . . . over vegetables in casserole.

Brown . . . . . . chicken lightly in skillet.

Drain . . . . . . chicken and place over vegetables.

Top . . . . with tomato slices.

Add . . . . heated broth and seasonings.

Bake . . . . at 350 degrees for 2 hours or until tender.

Yields . . . . . . 6-8 servings.

Helen Price
Pueblo, Colorado

 Substitute meat or vegetable juices for milk in sauces.

APPLE CIDER CHICKEN

1 3-lb. broiler-fryer, cut up
Flour
1/4 c. salad oil
1 sm. onion, sliced
1/2 clove of garlic, minced
1 env. chicken broth mix
Salt and pepper to taste
1/2 c. apple cider
2 tbsp. catsup
1 tsp. grated lemon rind

Coat . . . . chicken in flour.

Brown . . . . . . in hot oil in skillet.

Remove . . . . and drain.

Saute . . . . . . onion and garlic in pan drippings until tender.

Blend . . . . . . in 2 tablespoons flour, broth mix and seasonings.

Add . . . . remaining ingredients with 1/2 cup water.

Simmer . . . . . until thickened, stirring constantly.

Return . . . . . chicken to skillet.

Simmer . . . . . covered, for 45 minutes or until tender.

Serve . . . . with noodles.

Yields . . . . . . 4 servings.

Darla Jo Black
Harrisonville, Pennsylvania

CREPES FLORENTINE

1 3/4 c. flour
1 1/2 tsp. salt
3 1/2 c. milk
3 eggs, beaten
1/4 c. butter, melted
1 tsp. dry mustard
1 tsp. Worcestershire sauce
1   10-oz. package frozen spinach, cooked,
   drained
2 c. cooked diced chicken
1 c. sharp American cheese, shredded

Sift . . . . 1 1/2 cups flour and 1/2 teaspoon salt together into bowl.
Mix . . . . 1 1/2 cups milk with eggs.
Add . . . . to flour mixture, beating until
smooth.
Pour . . . . a small amount of batter into
hot greased 7-inch skillet ro-
tating to spread batter.
Brown . . . . . . on both sides.
Stack . . . . . . cooked crepes between sheets of
waxed paper.
Blend . . . . . . remaining 1/4 cup flour and 1
teaspoon salt into butter in
saucepan.
Add . . . . remaining 2 cups milk, mustard
and Worcestershire sauce.
Simmer . . . . . until thick, stirring constantly.
Combine . . . . 3/4 cup sauce, spinach and
chicken in bowl, mixing well.
Fill . . . . each crepe with chicken
mixture.
Roll . . . . and place seam side down in 9 x
13-inch baking dish.
Cover . . . . . . with remaining sauce.
Top . . . . with cheese.
Bake . . . . at 350 degrees for 20 minutes or
until bubbly.

Mary King
Raleigh, North Carolina

CHICKEN CHOW MEIN

2 c. sliced Chinese cabbage
3 c. thinly sliced celery
1   20-oz. can bean sprouts, drained
1   4-oz. can sliced water chestnuts
2 tsp. sugar
Salt and pepper to taste

2 c. chicken stock
2 1/2 tbsp. cornstarch
1/4 c. soy sauce
2 c. shredded cooked chicken
Chow mein noodles

Combine . . . . first 7 ingredients in saucepan,
mixing well.
Blend . . . . . . cornstarch and soy sauce with
1/4 cup cold water.
Add . . . . to vegetable mixture.
Simmer . . . . . until thickened, stirring
constantly.
Add . . . . chicken, heating to serving
temperature.
Serve . . . . over chow mein noodles.
Yields . . . . . . 4 servings.

Dera Leonard
Bangor, Maine

CHICKEN FRANCAIS

1   3 to 4-lb. chicken, cut up
1 tbsp. oil
1 lg. onion, chopped
2 cloves of garlic, chopped
1   1-lb. can tomatoes
1 c. chicken broth
1 c. julienne ham strips
1/2 tsp. Tabasco sauce
1/2 tsp. cinnamon
Pinch each of cloves, nutmeg
4 lg. carrots, cut into 1-in. pieces
1 bunch scallions, cut into 2-in. pieces

Brown . . . . . . chicken in oil in skillet; remove
chicken.
Saute . . . . . . onion and garlic in pan drippings
until golden; drain.
Add . . . . tomatoes, broth, ham, Tabasco
sauce and spices, mixing well.
Place . . . . chicken in skillet.
Simmer . . . . . covered, for 15 minutes.
Add . . . . carrots and scallions.
Cook . . . . covered, for 10 minutes longer
or until chicken is tender.
Remove . . . . chicken and vegetables to heated
serving platter; keep warm.
Cook . . . . pan juices over high heat until
reduced by half.
Spoon . . . . . . over chicken.
Yields . . . . . . 4 servings.

Photograph for this recipe on page 63.

LEMON CHICKEN BROIL

1   2 1/2 to 3-lb. chicken, quartered
Salt and pepper to taste
1/3 c. oil
1/4 c. lemon juice
1 clove of garlic, minced
1 tsp. finely chopped parsley

Place . . . . chicken, skin side up, on broiler rack.
Season . . . . . with salt and pepper.
Combine . . . . remaining ingredients.
Baste . . . . chicken with mixture.
Broil . . . . 4 inches from heat source for 12 minutes or until brown, basting frequently.
Turn . . . . chicken with tongs.
Continue . . . . to broil, basting frequently until brown and tender.

Marlys Hauck-Fenner
Freeman, South Dakota

SIMPLE CHICKEN-MACARONI

2 slices bacon, finely cut
1/3 c. minced onion
1/2 c. minced green pepper
2 c. shredded American cheese
1/4 c. chopped pimento
1/4 c. toasted sliced almonds
1 3/4 c. cooked drained peas
2 c. cut-up cooked chicken
1   8-oz. package macaroni, cooked, drained
Chicken broth

Cook . . . . bacon in large skillet until brown and crisp.
Remove . . . . and drain.
Saute . . . . . . onion and green pepper in pan drippings.
Add . . . . bacon and remaining ingredients with enough broth to moisten.
Heat . . . . to serving temperature.

Alice Watt
Wenrack, New York

CHICKEN VEGETABLE MEDLEY

1   3 1/2 to 4-lb. stewing chicken, cut up
Salt and pepper to taste
1/8 tsp. garlic powder
1/4 c. chopped parsley
4 lg. leeks, coarsely chopped
3 carrots, coarsely chopped
4 stalks celery with leaves, coarsely chopped
1 1/2 lb. fresh broccoli, coarsely chopped
1 green pepper, coarsely chopped
18 lg. button mushrooms
2 tbsp. cornstarch

Combine . . . . chicken with seasonings and 2 cups water in large saucepan.
Simmer . . . . . covered, for 1 1/2 hours.
Add . . . . vegetables, cooking 10 minutes or until tender.
Blend . . . . . . cornstarch with enough cold water to make a smooth paste.
Stir . . . . into chicken mixture.
Simmer . . . . . until thickened, stirring constantly.

Olive R. Curtis
Deming, Washington

GLAZED CORNISH HENS

2 tbsp. honey
2 tbsp. unsalted margarine, melted
Orange juice
4 Rock Cornish hens
1/4 c. chopped celery
1/4 c. chopped onion
2 tbsp. chopped parsley
1 tsp. grated orange peel
1/8 tsp. rosemary leaves, crushed
1/8 tsp. thyme leaves, crushed
1 c. Planters dry-roasted unsalted peanuts
1 c. rice

Combine . . . . first 2 ingredients with 2 tablespoons orange juice in small bowl.
Place . . . . Cornish hens on rack in baking pan.
Bake . . . . at 375 degrees for 1 hour or until tender, basting frequently with honey mixture.
Saute . . . . . . celery and onion in saucepan until tender.
Add . . . . remaining ingredients with 1/2 cup orange juice and 1 1/2 cups water.
Simmer . . . . . covered, until liquid is absorbed.
Place . . . . Cornish hens on serving plate surrounded by seasoned rice.

June Alley
Bridgeport, Connecticut

APRICOT-TURKEY KABOBS

1 env. creamy French salad dressing mix
1/3 c. dry white wine
1/4 c. wine vinegar
1/4 c. oil
1 30-oz. can apricot halves, drained
1 sm. green pepper, cut into chunks
1/2 pt. cherry tomatoes
2 c. cubed cooked turkey

Combine .... first 4 ingredients in shallow dish, mixing well.
Alternate ... apricots, green pepper, tomatoes and turkey on skewers.
Place .... in marinade, turning to coat.
Chill .... covered, for 4 hours or longer, turning occasionally.
Grill .... over hot coals until heated through. May be served cold.

Photograph for this recipe above.

 Marinades need no oil. Acid liquids will tenderize the meat fibers.

TURKEY CHOP SUEY

1 1-lb. can bean sprouts
1/2 c. sliced onions
1 1/2 to 2 c. diced cooked turkey
1 c. sliced celery
1 6-oz. can sliced water chestnuts, drained
1/2 c. turkey broth
2 tbsp. cornstarch
1/4 tsp. salt

1/4 tsp. monosodium glutamate
2 tbsp. soy sauce
4 c. hot cooked rice
1/2 c. blanched slivered almonds, toasted

Drain ...... bean sprouts, reserving liquid.
Saute ...... onions in saucepan until tender.
Add .... next 4 ingredients and reserved liquid.
Combine .... cornstarch with seasonings, 1/4 cup water and soy sauce in bowl, mixing well.
Stir .... into turkey mixture.
Simmer ..... until thickened, stirring constantly.
Add .... bean sprouts, stirring until heated.
Serve .... over rice.
Garnish ..... with almonds.
Yields ...... 4-6 servings.

Jean Beaty
Akron, Ohio

TURKEY DIVAN

2 tbsp. unsalted margarine
2 tbsp. flour
1 1/4 c. milk
1 egg yolk, slightly beaten
1/4 tsp. dry mustard
1/4 tsp. salt substitute
Pepper to taste
1/4 c. grated low-sodium cheese
2 10-oz. packages frozen broccoli, cooked, drained
6 servings sliced cooked turkey
2 tbsp. grated Parmesan cheese

Combine .... first 4 ingredients in saucepan, blending well.
Simmer ..... until thickened, stirring constantly.
Stir .... in seasonings and low-sodium cheese until cheese melts.
Layer ...... hot broccoli and turkey with cheese sauce in 12 x 8-inch baking dish, ending with sauce.
Sprinkle .... Parmesan cheese over top.
Broil .... 4 inches from heat source until cheese browns.
Yields ...... 6 servings.

Catherine S. Stroube
Nashville, Tennessee

egg &
cheese

EASY EGG CASSEROLE

3 tbsp. margarine, melted
2 tbsp. flour
1/4 tsp. salt
1 c. skim milk
1 c. grated cheese
2 c. cracker crumbs
3 hard-cooked eggs, sliced

Blend ...... first 3 ingredients in saucepan.
Stir .... in milk and cheese.
Cook .... over medium heat until thick, stirring constantly.
Layer ...... 1 cup crumbs, eggs and sauce in 8 x 8-inch baking dish.
Top .... with remaining crumbs.
Bake .... at 350 degrees until bubbly.
Yields ...... 6 servings.

Ruby Carver
Nacogdoches, Texas

CHEESE AND EGG PUFF

Margarine
1/2 c. pancake mix
12 eggs
1/4 c. chopped green onions
1 1/2 c. shredded sharp Cheddar cheese
2 to 3 tbsp. chopped pimento

Bring .... 1/4 cup margarine and 1/2 cup water to a boil in medium saucepan.
Add .... pancake mix, stirring until dough forms ball; remove from heat.
Add .... 2 eggs, 1 at a time, beating well after each addition.
Spread ..... evenly in greased pie plate.
Bake .... at 400 degrees for 15 to 18 minutes.
Mix .... remaining eggs, onions, cheese and pimento in bowl.
Melt .... a small amount of margarine in large skillet.
Pour .... in egg mixture.
Cook .... over low heat, stirring to scramble.
Spoon ...... eggs into center of puff and serve immediately.

Ruth Larson
Columbia, Missouri

MUSHROOM-EGG CASSEROLE

2 tbsp. butter, melted
2 tbsp. flour
1 8-oz. can mushrooms
1 2/3 c. evaporated skim milk
3/4 c. grated cheese
8 hard-boiled eggs, sliced
Buttered bread crumbs

Blend ...... butter and flour in saucepan.
Drain ...... mushrooms, reserving 2 tablespoons liquid.
Stir .... milk and mushroom liquid into flour mixture gradually.
Cook .... until smooth and thick, stirring constantly.
Add .... cheese, stirring until melted.
Layer ...... half the eggs, mushrooms and sauce in greased baking dish.
Repeat ..... layers with remaining ingredients.
Top .... with crumbs.
Bake .... at 350 degrees for 40 minutes.
Yields ...... 8 servings.

Susan Grand
Beaver Creek, Washington

ORIENTAL EGGS

4 eggs, beaten
3/4 c. each finely chopped onions, green peppers
1 c. fresh bean sprouts
Salt to taste
Soy sauce to taste
1 tbsp. (heaping) nonfat dry milk
1 tbsp. (heaping) soy powder
2 tbsp. safflower oil

Combine .... all ingredients except oil in bowl, mixing well.
Drop .... by tablespoonfuls into oil in skillet.
Saute ...... until browned on both sides.
Yields ...... 2 servings.

Nancy Dunn
Roanoke, Virginia

HEALTH NUT OMELET

3 soft corn tortillas, cut up
Butter

1 sm. onion, chopped
6 eggs, beaten
1/2 green pepper, chopped
1/4 c. grated cheese
1 tomato, chopped
1 tbsp. sunflower seed
1 tbsp. bacon bits
2 tbsp. alfalfa sprouts

Brown . . . . . tortillas in butter in skillet.
Add . . . . onion.
Saute . . . . . . until tender-crisp.
Pour . . . . eggs over top.
Sprinkle . . . . with green pepper and cheese.
Cook . . . . over low heat until partially set.
Top . . . . with remaining ingredients.
Cook . . . . until set.

Susan Stanley
Keene, New Hampshire

MUSHROOM OMELET

1 egg, beaten
1 tsp. Picante Sauce
1/4 c. sliced mushrooms
2 tbsp. nonfat dry milk
1 tsp. bacon bits
Salt and pepper to taste

Combine . . . . all ingredients in bowl, mixing well.
Pour . . . . into nonstick omelet pan.
Cook . . . . until brown; fold in half.
Yields . . . . . . 1 serving.

Susan Inglis
Corpus Christi, Texas

MUSHROOM AND SPINACH FRITTATA

1 8-oz. can mushrooms, drained
1/2 c. chopped onion
1 tbsp. each olive oil, margarine
1 10-oz. package frozen chopped spinach, thawed
6 eggs, beaten
2 tbsp. Parmesan cheese
1 tbsp. chopped parsley
3/4 tsp. salt
1/2 tsp. Italian seasoning

Saute . . . . . . mushrooms and onion in olive oil and margarine in skillet for 5 minutes.

Stir . . . . in spinach.
Combine . . . . remaining ingredients in bowl, mixing well.
Pour . . . . over mushroom mixture, mixing well.
Cook . . . . over medium heat until edge is golden brown and center is firm.
Turn . . . . onto warm platter and cut into wedges.

Photograph for this recipe above.

 Breakfast is a healthy habit.

SPANISH OMELETS WITH HAM

1 sm. can tomato sauce
1 sm. onion, chopped
1/2 green pepper, chopped
1 stalk celery, chopped
Salt and pepper to taste
1 sm. can English peas
6 eggs, beaten
1/2 c. chopped cooked ham

Simmer . . . . . first 6 ingredients in saucepan until thick, stirring occasionally.
Stir . . . . in peas.
Cook . . . . eggs, 1/2 at a time, in skillet as for omelet.
Slide . . . . omelets onto serving plate.
Sprinkle . . . . ham over half the omelets.
Spoon . . . . . . sauce over ham; fold omelets in half.
Serve . . . . with remaining sauce.
Yields . . . . . . 6 servings.

Susan O'Connor
Kingston, West Virginia

SPANISH VEGETABLE OMELET

1/2 c. finely chopped onion
1 tbsp. olive oil
2 tbsp. butter, melted
2 sm. tomatoes, peeled, seeded, chopped
1 med. green pepper, chopped
1/4 c. chopped pimento-stuffed olives
1 tbsp. chopped parsley
1/2 tsp. salt
8 eggs, beaten

Saute . . . . . . onion in olive oil and 1 table-spoon butter in skillet until tender.
Add . . . . tomatoes and green pepper.
Cook . . . . until green pepper is tender; drain.
Stir . . . . vegetable mixture, olives, parsley and salt into eggs.
Pour . . . . into 1 tablespoon butter in omelet pan.
Cook . . . . over low heat until almost firm, lifting edge occasionally.
Invert . . . . . . onto plate, then return to omelet pan.
Cook . . . . until lightly browned.
Invert . . . . . . on serving plate; garnish with olives and watercress.
Yields . . . . . . 4 servings.

Photograph for this recipe on page 75.

FOOD PROCESSOR CHEESE SOUFFLE

6 eggs
1/2 c. evaporated skim milk
1/4 c. grated Parmesan cheese
1/2 tsp. prepared mustard
1/2 tsp. salt
1/4 tsp. pepper
1/2 lb. sharp Cheddar cheese, shredded
11 oz. cream cheese, cubed

Attach . . . . . steel blade to food processor.
Combine . . . . eggs, milk, Parmesan cheese, mustard, salt and pepper in processor container.
Process . . . . . mixture until smooth.
Add . . . . Cheddar cheese and cream cheese while processor is running.

Process . . . . . until cheeses are blended, then for 5 seconds longer.
Pour . . . . into buttered souffle dish.
Bake . . . . at 375 degrees for 45 to 50 minutes.

Joan Madison
Portland, Oregon

HEALTH CASSEROLE

3 eggs, beaten
1 lb. small curd low-fat cottage cheese
3 c. Special K cereal
1/2 c. low-calorie margarine, melted
1/2 c. dry onion soup mix
1/2 c. chopped walnuts
2 tbsp. protein powder
1/4 c. wheat germ

Combine . . . . all ingredients in bowl, mixing well.
Spoon . . . . . . into lightly greased casserole.
Bake . . . . at 350 degrees for 50 minutes.

Sandra Davis
Tucson, Arizona

MEXICAN RAREBIT

2 eggs
1/2 c. chopped tomatoes
2 tbsp. safflower oil
1 sm. green pepper, chopped
1 1/2 c. grated Cheddar cheese
1 c. whole kernel corn
1/2 c. nonfat dry milk
1/4 c. wheat germ
Salt to taste
1 tsp. chili powder
1/2 c. soy powder

Combine . . . . first 6 ingredients in large saucepan, mixing well.
Heat . . . . to simmering.
Mix . . . . remaining dry ingredients in bowl.
Add . . . . gradually to vegetable mixture, stirring constantly.
Simmer . . . . . for 15 minutes or until thick, stirring frequently.
Yields . . . . . . 6 servings.

Susan Samson
Saratoga, Florida

PIZZA ON A MUFFIN

1 tbsp. finely chopped onion
2 tbsp. tomato paste
1/4 tsp. each basil, oregano
1/8 tsp. garlic powder
1 English muffin, halved, toasted
2 tbsp. mushrooms
2 oz. shredded mozzarella cheese

Saute ...... onion in skillet until tender.
Add .... tomato paste, spices and 1/4 cup water, mixing well.
Cook ...... until thickened, stirring occasionally.
Spoon ...... tomato mixture onto muffin halves.
Top .... with mushrooms and cheese.
Place .... on baking sheet.
Broil .... for 5 minutes or until cheese melts.

Doris Stiles
Louisville, Kentucky

CHEESE AND EGG CROWN CASSEROLE

7 slices bread
Margarine, softened
1 c. grated sharp cheese
3 eggs, lightly beaten
2 c. milk
Salt to taste
1/2 tsp. dry mustard
1/8 tsp. each white pepper, garlic powder

Spread ..... bread with a small amount of margarine.
Cut .... 2 slices into 4 triangles and cube remaining slices.
Place .... half the bread cubes in greased 1-quart casserole.
Top .... with cheese and remaining bread cubes.
Arrange ..... bread triangles, pointed sides up, around edge.
Combine .... remaining ingredients in bowl, mixing well.
Pour .... over bread.
Place .... in pan of hot water.
Bake .... at 325 degrees for 1 hour.
Yields ...... 6 servings.

Liz Fayette
Bicknell, North Carolina

COTTAGE CHEESE DUMPLINGS

1 tbsp. chopped onion
1 pt. dry cottage cheese
4 egg yolks, beaten
Salt to taste
2 c. flour
2 egg whites
Milk

Saute ...... onion in skillet until tender.
Combine .... with cottage cheese, egg yolks and salt in bowl, mixing well; set aside.
Mix .... flour, salt and egg whites with enough milk in bowl to make stiff dough.
Roll .... 1/4 inch thick on floured surface.
Cut .... into 3-inch squares.
Place .... 2 tablespoons cottage cheese mixture in center of each square.
Fold .... squares in half, sealing edges.
Drop .... into boiling salted water in saucepan.
Cook .... for 5 minutes; drain.
Yields ...... 4 servings.

Diane Todd
Bagley, South Carolina

TOMATO-CHEESE SOUFFLE

2 tbsp. margarine
2 tbsp. flour
1 c. tomato juice, scalded
Salt to taste
Dash of pepper
1/2 c. shredded Cheddar cheese
4 eggs, separated

Blend ...... margarine and flour in saucepan until smooth.
Stir .... in tomato juice gradually.
Add .... salt, pepper and cheese.
Cook .... until cheese melts, stirring constantly; remove from heat.
Add .... slightly beaten egg yolks, mixing well.
Fold .... in stiffly beaten egg whites.
Spoon ...... into casserole.
Place .... in pan of hot water.
Bake .... at 350 degrees for 45 minutes.

Crystal Cates
Dover, Delaware

MUSHROOM-CHEESE TART

1 c. each sliced onion, mushrooms
1 unbaked 9-in. whole wheat pie shell
1/2 c. grated Swiss cheese
3 eggs, well beaten
3/4 c. evaporated skim milk
Salt to taste
1/8 tsp. pepper

Saute ...... onion and mushrooms in skillet for 5 minutes.
Spread ..... in pie shell.
Sprinkle .... cheese over top.
Combine .... remaining ingredients in bowl, mixing well.
Pour .... over cheese.
Bake .... at 375 degrees for 45 minutes.
Yields ...... 4 servings.

Dorothy Trenton
Little Rock, Arkansas

CHEESE-ONION QUICHE

1 c. crushed whole wheat crackers
3 tbsp. margarine, softened
3 c. thinly sliced onions
1 1/4 c. milk, scalded
3 eggs, beaten
Salt to taste
1/4 lb. Cheddar cheese, grated

Combine .... crumbs and margarine in bowl, mixing well.
Press .... into 9-inch pie plate.
Saute ...... onions in skillet until tender.
Spread ..... in prepared crust.
Stir .... a small amount of hot milk into eggs; stir eggs into hot milk.
Add .... salt and 1/2 of the cheese, stirring until melted.
Pour .... over onions.
Top .... with remaining cheese.
Bake .... at 325 degrees for 45 minutes.
Yields ...... 6 servings.

Hazel Henry
Torrance, California

HAM AND CHEESE QUICHE

1 c. chopped cooked ham
1 med. onion, grated
1 tsp. butter
1 unbaked pie shell
1/2 c. grated Swiss cheese
4 eggs, beaten
1 1/2 c. evaporated skim milk
1 c. milk
Salt and pepper to taste
Pinch of nutmeg

Saute ...... ham and onion in butter in skillet for 5 minutes.
Place .... in pie shell with cheese.
Combine .... remaining ingredients, mixing well.
Pour .... into shell.
Bake .... at 450 degrees for 15 minutes.
Reduce ..... temperature to 350 degrees.
Bake .... for 15 to 20 minutes longer or until custard is set.

Lorena Wigger
Anamasa, Iowa

NO-CRUST QUICHE

5 or 6 eggs
Salt, lemon-pepper marinade to taste
1/4 c. chopped jalapeno peppers
1/2 to 3/4 c. grated Cheddar cheese

Beat .... eggs with seasonings in bowl.
Layer ...... peppers, cheese and egg mixture in buttered casserole.
Bake .... at 350 degrees for 25 minutes or until firm.

Ann Morton
Arlington, Virginia

MUSHROOM PILAF

1 c. wheat pilaf
4 tbsp. safflower oil
1/2 c. soy grits
4 stalks celery, chopped
2 onions, chopped
1 clove of garlic, minced
1/4 c. soy powder
4 ripe tomatoes, chopped
4 tbsp. Worcestershire sauce
Salt to taste
1 tsp. paprika
1/2 tsp. thyme
2 c. chopped mushrooms
1/2 c. skim milk cottage cheese

Saute ...... pilaf in oil in skillet for 1 minute, stirring constantly.

Add . . . . soy grits and 2 1/2 cups water.
Simmer . . . . . covered, for 15 minutes.
Add . . . . remaining ingredients except cottage cheese.
Simmer . . . . . for 30 minutes longer.
Stir . . . . in cottage cheese.
Cook . . . . for 10 minutes longer, stirring constantly.
Yields . . . . . . 4 servings.

Judy Blumburg
Canton, Ohio

BROWN RICE SOUFFLE

4 eggs, separated
1/4 c. cooked brown rice
1/4 c. finely chopped onion
3/4 c. skim milk
Salt to taste
1 tbsp. Worcestershire sauce
Dash of Tabasco sauce
1/4 tsp. paprika
2 tbsp. safflower oil
1 c. grated carrot
1/4 c. nonfat dry milk
1/4 c. soy powder
1 c. grated American cheese

Combine . . . . beaten egg yolks and next 9 ingredients in saucepan, mixing well.
Bring . . . . to a boil, stirring constantly.
Stir . . . . in dry milk, soy powder and cheese.
Cook . . . . until cheese melts, stirring constantly; remove from heat.
Fold . . . . in stiffly beaten egg whites.
Pour . . . . into oiled 1-quart baking dish.
Bake . . . . at 300 degrees for 45 minutes or until browned.
Yields . . . . . . 4 servings.

Louise Lewis
Kingston, Pennsylvania

GREEN RICE

1 c. chopped parsley
4 green onions with tops, chopped
1 c. chopped celery
5 c. cooked rice
1 1/2 c. milk
2 eggs, beaten
1 can consomme
1 c. grated Cheddar cheese

Salt and pepper to taste
Poultry seasoning to taste

Saute . . . . . . parsley, onions and celery in skillet until tender.
Combine . . . . with remaining ingredients in bowl, mixing well.
Spoon . . . . . . into greased 3-quart baking dish.
Bake . . . . at 350 degrees for 40 minutes.

Georgina Barker
Bristol, Tennessee

GOLDEN RICE BAKE

2 c. grated American cheese
2 c. cooked rice
3 c. shredded carrots
1/2 c. milk
2 eggs, beaten
2 tbsp. minced onion
1 1/2 tsp. salt
1/4 tsp. pepper

Combine . . . . 1 1/2 cups cheese with remaining ingredients in bowl, mixing well.
Pour . . . . into greased 1 1/2-quart baking dish.
Sprinkle . . . . with remaining 1/2 cup cheese.
Bake . . . . at 350 degrees for 1 hour.
Yields . . . . . . 6 servings.

Jenifer Johnson
Fort Lee, Virginia

PRINCESS LOAF

2 tbsp. chopped onion
2 tbsp. soy sauce
1 c. tomato puree
1/2 c. evaporated skim milk
2 c. cooked rice
1 c. fine bread crumbs
1/2 c. ground walnuts
2 eggs, beaten
Salt to taste

Saute . . . . . . onion in skillet until tender.
Add . . . . next 6 ingredients, mixing well.
Stir . . . . in eggs and salt.
Spoon . . . . . . into greased baking dish.
Bake . . . . at 350 degrees for 45 minutes.
Yields . . . . . . 6 servings.

Gail Hughes
Senatoba, Mississippi

RICE-CHEESE CASSEROLE

2 c. cooked rice
2 eggs, beaten
2 c. milk
3 c. grated sharp Cheddar cheese
3 lg. onions, chopped
2 cloves of garlic, minced
1 c. minced parsley
2 lg. green peppers, chopped
1 lg. can mushrooms, drained
Salt and pepper to taste

Combine .... all ingredients in large greased casserole.
Bake .... at 350 degrees for 1 1/4 hours.
Yields ...... 8 servings.

Andrea Preston
North Little Rock, Arkansas

WILD RICE WITH ALMONDS

1   8-oz. can mushroom pieces, drained
1 clove of garlic
2 tbsp. each chopped green pepper,
   green onion
1/2 c. slivered almonds
1/2 c. butter
1 c. wild rice
3 c. chicken broth
Salt and pepper to taste

Saute ...... first 5 ingredients in butter in skillet for 5 minutes.
Add .... rice.
Saute ...... until rice is golden.
Stir .... in remaining ingredients.
Pour .... into buttered casserole.
Bake .... covered, at 325 degrees for 1 hour or until rice is tender.

Cara Josten
Mitchellville, Iowa

MACARONI AND CHEESE SUPREME

1 sm. onion, finely chopped
1   8-oz. package macaroni, cooked
1/2 c. yogurt
1 c. cottage cheese
1 egg, beaten
Salt
1/4 tsp. pepper
6 oz. sharp Cheddar cheese, cubed

Saute ...... onion in skillet until tender.
Combine .... with macaroni in 2-quart casserole.
Add .... remaining ingredients, mixing well.
Bake .... at 325 degrees for 1 hour.
Cool .... for 5 minutes before serving.
Yields ...... 5-6 servings.

June Delta
Belle, Florida

PIZZA CASSEROLE

2 c. cooked elbow macaroni
1/2 lb. Cheddar cheese, grated
2 c. tomatoes, chopped
1 tsp. oregano
1/8 tsp. garlic powder
1 tsp. instant minced onions
1/4 lb. mozzarella cheese, grated

Layer ...... macaroni and Cheddar cheese alternately in 2-quart baking dish until all ingredients are used.
Combine .... tomatoes and seasonings in bowl, mixing well.
Pour .... tomato mixture over macaroni and cheese.
Bake .... covered, at 400 degrees for 45 minutes.
Sprinkle .... mozzarella cheese over top.
Bake .... uncovered, for 15 minutes longer.
Yields ...... 4 servings.

Dorothy S. Weirick
Salt Lake City, Utah

MACARONI NUT CASSEROLE

Salt
1   8-oz. package elbow macaroni
2 tbsp. salad oil
1/4 c. sesame seed
4 eggs, beaten
1/3 c. chopped onion
1 1/2 c. chopped celery
1 c. chopped cashews
1 c. chopped walnuts
1 lb. creamed cottage cheese
2 tbsp. chopped chives
1/4 c. chopped parsley
1 1/2 tsp. sea salt
1/4 tsp. pepper

1 tsp. grated onion
1/2 green pepper, chopped

Combine .... macaroni, milk, beaten egg yolks, bread cubes, cheese, onion and green pepper in bowl, mixing well.
Fold .... in stiffly beaten egg whites.
Pour .... into casserole.
Bake .... at 350 degrees for 1/2 hour.

Marta Range
South Bend, Indiana

BAKED NOODLES ROMANOFF

1   8-oz. package med. egg noodles, cooked
1/4 c. margarine, melted
1/4 c. yogurt
1 c. cottage cheese
1 sm. onion, minced
Dash of garlic salt
Salt and pepper to taste
1/2 c. grated Cheddar cheese
2 tbsp. fine dry bread crumbs

Combine .... noodles and margarine in bowl, mixing well.
Stir .... in yogurt, cottage cheese, onion and seasonings.
Turn .... into 2-quart casserole.
Sprinkle .... cheese and crumbs over top.
Bake .... at 350 degrees for 40 minutes.
Yields ...... 6 servings.

Evie Wallace
Bloomingdale, Ohio

NOODLE LOAF

2 c. noodles, cooked, drained
1 1/2 c. milk
1 c. bread crumbs
2 tbsp. butter
3 eggs, beaten
1 tbsp. minced onion
2 tbsp. minced parsley
3/4 lb. cheese, cubed
1 1/2 tsp. salt

Combine .... all ingredients in casserole, mixing well.
Bake .... at 350 degrees for 1 hour.
Yields ...... 10 servings.

Claudia Page
Smithville, Ohio

1/2 tsp. thyme leaves, crushed
1/4 c. wheat germ

Add .... 1 tablespoon salt to 3 quarts rapidly boiling water.
Stir .... in macaroni gradually so that water continues to boil.
Cook .... uncovered, until just tender, stirring occasionally; drain in colander.
Heat .... oil in small skillet.
Add .... sesame seed; stir until browned.
Combine .... eggs, remaining ingredients, macaroni and sesame seed in large bowl.
Toss .... lightly until combined.
Add .... salt to taste.
Spoon ...... into 2-quart casserole.
Bake .... in 375-degree oven for 50 to 55 minutes or until set.
Garnish ..... with parsley sprigs.

Photograph for this recipe above.

MACARONI MOUSSE

1 c. macaroni, cooked
1 c. milk, scalded
3 eggs, separated
1 c. bread cubes
1 c. finely shredded cheese

CHEESE-NOODLE CASSEROLE

1/4 c. melted margarine
3 tbsp. flour
Salt to taste
1/4 tsp. garlic salt
1/8 tsp. white pepper
Dash of nutmeg
2 c. milk
1/2 c. dry white wine
8 oz. Swiss cheese, shredded
1/2 c. Parmesan cheese
3 c. noodles, cooked, drained
2 tbsp. sliced green onion
2 tbsp. chopped pimento

Combine .... first 6 ingredients in saucepan, mixing well.
Stir .... in milk gradually.
Cook .... until thickened, stirring constantly.
Add .... wine and Swiss cheese, stirring until cheese melts.
Fold .... in 1/4 cup Parmesan cheese and remaining ingredients.
Turn .... into shallow 1 1/2-quart casserole.
Sprinkle .... with remaining Parmesan cheese.
Bake .... at 350 degrees for 25 minutes.

Phyllis Alicsen
Redford, California

MICROWAVE MANICOTTI

1 c. cottage cheese
1/2 c. grated mozzarella cheese
1/2 c. Parmesan cheese
1 egg
1/2 c. bread crumbs
1 tsp. Italian seasoning
1/2 c. grated Cheddar cheese
1 box manicotti noodles, cooked
3/4 c. tomato sauce

Combine .... first 6 ingredients with 1/4 cup Cheddar cheese in bowl, mixing well.
Stuff .... manicotti with mixture.
Place .... in greased 11 x 14-inch glass baking dish.
Top .... with tomato sauce and remaining Cheddar cheese.
Microwave .. on Medium for 8 minutes.

Amber Waters
Louisville, Kentucky

SPAGHETTI LOAF

2 tbsp. melted margarine
3 eggs, beaten
Salt to taste
Dash of pepper
1 c. grated cheese
1 green pepper, chopped
2 pimentos, chopped
1 tbsp. chopped parsley
1 c. milk
1 c. cooked spaghetti
1 c. white sauce

Combine .... all ingredients except white sauce, mixing well.
Turn .... into loaf pan.
Bake .... at 300 degrees for 45 minutes.
Serve .... with white sauce and additional grated cheese.

Sue Farlow
Fort Meade, Maryland

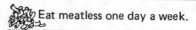 Eat meatless one day a week.

SPANISH SPAGHETTI

1 onion, chopped
1 tbsp. chili powder
Salt to taste
1/8 tsp. pepper
2 1/2 c. stewed tomatoes
3 c. cooked spaghetti
1 1/2 c. grated American cheese
1/4 c. chopped olives

Saute ...... onion in saucepan until lightly browned.
Stir .... in chili powder, salt and pepper.
Add .... tomatoes.
Simmer ..... for 20 minutes, stirring frequently.
Layer ...... spaghetti and cheese in casserole, reserving 1/2 cup cheese.
Pour .... sauce over top.
Sprinkle .... olives over sauce.
Top .... with remaining cheese.
Bake .... at 350 degrees until cheese melts.
Yields ...... 6 servings.

Louise Hatfill
Charter, Georgia

vegetables

STUFFED ARTICHOKES

1/4 c. chopped carrot
1/4 c. chopped onion
1/4 c. chopped celery
1/4 lb. fresh mushrooms, chopped
Salt to taste
1/8 tsp. pepper
2 tsp. fresh lemon juice
1/4 tsp. dried dillweed
4 artichokes, trimmed, cleaned

Saute ...... first 3 ingredients in skillet until tender.
Add .... mushrooms, salt, pepper, lemon juice and dillweed.
Cook .... for 10 minutes or until mushrooms are tender.
Spoon ...... into artichoke cavities.
Place .... in baking pan, adding 1/2 inch water to pan.
Bake .... covered, at 375 degrees for 45 minutes.
Yields ...... 4 servings.

Allene Gardner
Allington, New York

 Season vegetables with a squeeze of lemon juice.

ASPARAGUS SOUFFLE

3 tbsp. margarine
3 tbsp. flour
1 c. milk
4 eggs, separated
2 1/2 c. diced cooked asparagus
3/4 tsp. salt

Blend ...... margarine and flour in saucepan until smooth.
Stir .... in milk gradually.
Cook .... until thick, stirring constantly.
Combine .... beaten egg yolks, asparagus and salt in bowl.
Stir .... in white sauce gently.
Fold .... in stiffly beaten egg whites.
Pour .... into greased casserole.
Place .... in pan of hot water.
Bake .... at 325 degrees for 45 minutes or until firm.
Yields ...... 6 servings.

Judi Rea
Baker, Montana

STIR-FRY ASPARAGUS

2 lb. fresh asparagus, cut into 2-in. pieces
2 tbsp. margarine, melted
1/2 tsp. salt
1/8 tsp. pepper
1/2 tsp. dried thyme

Combine .... all ingredients in skillet.
Cook .... covered, over medium-high heat for 5 minutes or until tender-crisp, stirring occasionally.
Yields ...... 4-6 servings.

Christine Lawton
Rawlins, Florida

CREOLE GREEN BEANS

1/4 c. each chopped onion, celery, green pepper
1 20-oz. can tomatoes
Salt to taste
Pepper to taste
1 lb. fresh green beans, cooked, drained
3 slices crisp-cooked bacon, crumbled

Saute ...... onion, celery and green pepper in skillet until tender.
Stir .... in tomatoes, salt and pepper.
Simmer ..... for 5 mintues.
Add .... green beans, mixing well.
Simmer ..... for 5 minutes longer.
Spoon ...... into serving bowl.
Top .... with bacon.
Yields ...... 6 servings.

Joan Canfield
Austin, Texas

STIR-FRIED GREEN BEANS

8 oz. fresh mushrooms, sliced
1 lb. fresh green beans
4 strips crisp-cooked bacon, crumbled

Saute ...... mushrooms in skillet until tender; remove.
Saute ...... green beans until tender.
Combine .... green beans and mushrooms in serving bowl.
Top .... with bacon.

Candy Canfield
Stanford, Connecticut

BROCCOLI WITH ALMOND SAUCE

2 tbsp. melted margarine
2 1/2 tbsp. flour
1 1/4 c. skim milk
1/4 tsp. salt
Dash of cayenne pepper
2 egg yolks, slightly beaten
2 tbsp. lemon juice
1 1/2 lb. broccoli, cooked
1/3 c. toasted slivered almonds

Blend ...... margarine and flour in saucepan.
Stir .... in milk and seasonings gradually.
Cook .... until thick, stirring constantly.
Stir .... a small amount of hot mixture into egg yolks; stir egg yolks into hot mixture.
Cook .... for 3 to 4 minutes, stirring constantly. Do not boil.
Add .... lemon juice gradually, blending well.
Pour .... over broccoli.
Top .... with almonds.
Yields ...... 5-6 servings.

Sharon Templeton
Fairfield, Oregon

SCALLOPED BROCCOLI

3/4 c. evaporated skim milk
3/4 c. chopped onions
1 3-oz. can mushrooms, drained
1 tsp. salt
1/4 tsp. nutmeg
1/8 tsp. pepper
3 eggs, slightly beaten
1 10-oz. package frozen broccoli spears, cooked, drained

Combine .... first 6 ingredients in saucepan, mixing well.
Simmer ..... for 1 minute.
Stir .... a small amount of hot mixture into eggs; stir eggs into hot mixture.
Arrange ..... broccoli in greased baking dish.
Spoon ...... sauce over broccoli.
Bake .... at 350 degrees for 30 minutes or until knife inserted in center comes out clean.
Yields ...... 6 servings.

Margaret Henderson
Walters, Oklahoma

BRUSSELS SPROUTS AND WALNUTS AU GRATIN

2 10-oz. packages frozen Brussels sprouts, cooked, drained
1/2 c. grated process sharp cheese
1/4 c. herb-seasoned bread crumbs
1/3 c. chopped walnuts
2 tbsp. butter, melted

Place .... Brussels sprouts in greased casserole.
Sprinkle .... with cheese.
Toss .... crumbs and walnuts with butter.
Sprinkle .... over cheese.
Bake .... at 400 degrees for 10 minutes or until cheese melts.
Yields ...... 6 servings.

Phyllis White
Pueblo, Colorado

BAKED CABBAGE

3 c. shredded cabbage, cooked
1 1/2 c. drained canned tomatoes
Salt and paprika to taste
1 c. grated cheese
1 c. bread crumbs
1 tbsp. butter

Alternate ... layers of cabbage and tomatoes in greased casserole, sprinkling each layer with salt and paprika.
Top .... with cheese and bread crumbs.
Dot .... with butter.
Bake .... at 300 degrees for 15 minutes or until cheese melts.
Yields ...... 6 servings.

Fran Osbourne
Marcus, Minnesota

CARROTS A LA ORANGE

1 11-oz. can mandarin oranges
1 lb. small carrots, sliced
2 tbsp. unsalted butter

Drain ...... oranges, reserving juice.
Cook .... carrots in reserved juice in saucepan until tender; drain well.
Stir .... in butter and oranges.
Heat .... to serving temperature.
Yields ...... 4-6 servings.

Arlene Craft
Lawton, Oklahoma

SAUTEED CARROTS AND ZUCCHINI

6 med. carrots, slivered
1 bunch green onions, coarsely chopped
3 med. zucchini, slivered
1/2 tsp. salt

Saute ...... carrots and onions in skillet for 3 minutes.
Add .... zucchini and salt.
Saute ...... for 3 minutes or until zucchini is tender-crisp.

Emily Lewis
Oklahoma City, Oklahoma

CAULIFLOWER PARMESAN

1 med. cauliflower, separated
1 1/2 tsp. salt
1 tsp. lemon juice (opt.)
1 sm. clove of garlic, minced
2 tbsp. olive oil
8 to 10 tomato wedges
1 tsp. chopped parsley
2 tbsp. grated Parmesan cheese

Cook .... cauliflowerets in water to cover with 1 teaspoon salt and lemon juice for 10 minutes or until tender-crisp; drain well.
Saute ...... garlic in olive oil in skillet until brown.
Add .... cauliflowerets.
Saute ...... lightly.
Add .... tomatoes and remaining 1/2 teaspoon salt, mixing gently.
Simmer ..... covered, for 2 to 3 minutes.
Spoon ...... into serving dish.
Top .... with parsley and cheese.

Artes Proctor
Garden City, Kansas

LOW-CALORIE CURRIED CAULIFLOWER

1 pkg. frozen cauliflower, cooked, drained
1/4 tsp. curry powder

Sprinkle .... cauliflower with curry powder.
Serve .... immediately.
Yields ...... 4 servings.

Mary Weaver
Batavia, Pennsylvania

CELERY PARMIGIANA

4 c. sliced celery
1/4 c. chopped onion
1/2 clove of garlic, minced
Salt to taste
4 slices crisp-cooked bacon, crumbled
2 tomatoes, chopped
1 c. Parmesan cheese

Combine .... first 4 ingredients with 1 cup water in saucepan.
Simmer ..... covered, for 20 minutes or until tender; drain.
Layer ...... cooked vegetables, bacon, tomatoes and cheese in casserole.
Bake .... at 350 degrees for 15 minutes.

Photograph for this recipe above.

FRENCH-BRAISED CELERY

2 c. coarsely chopped celery
4 sprigs of parsley
4 slices onion
1/2 c. bouillon
1 tsp. salt
1/4 tsp. pepper
2 strips crisp-cooked bacon, crumbled
Buttered bread crumbs

Combine .... first 6 ingredients in casserole.
Bake .... covered, at 375 degrees for 30 minutes.
Sprinkle .... with bacon and crumbs.
Bake .... uncovered, for 10 minutes longer or until brown.
Yields ...... 4 servings.

Mary Ann Hribek
Giddings, Texas

DIETER'S COOKED CUCUMBERS

1 chicken bouillon cube
1 tbsp. butter
2 lg. cucumbers, peeled, sliced

Combine .... bouillon cube and butter with 1/4 cup water in saucepan.
Bring .... to a boil.
Add .... cucumbers.
Simmer ..... covered, for 10 minutes or until tender; drain.
Serve .... immediately.
Yields ...... 2-3 servings.

Dot Baxter
Langton, Louisiana

BAKED EGGPLANT PARMESAN

1 eggplant, cooked, mashed
2 tbsp. butter
1/2 tsp. salt
1/4 tsp. pepper
1/2 c. bread crumbs
Parmesan cheese

Combine .... all ingredients except cheese, mixing well.
Spoon ...... into lightly greased 8-inch baking dish.
Sprinkle .... with cheese.
Bake .... at 350 degrees for 20 minutes or until bubbly.

Beth Kelso
Jackson, Michigan

EGGPLANT SOUFFLE

1 eggplant, pierced
1/4 c. wheat germ
1/4 c. soy powder
2 tbsp. safflower oil
1 onion, chopped
Salt
1/4 tsp. pepper
1/2 tsp. coriander seed
2 eggs, separated
3/4 c. skim milk
2 tbsp. (heaping) nonfat dry milk

Place .... eggplant in baking dish.
Bake .... at 400 degrees for 45 minutes.
Peel .... and mash eggplant in bowl.

Add .... next 7 ingredients.
Combine .... egg yolks with remaining ingredients in bowl, mixing well.
Stir .... into eggplant.
Fold .... in stiffly beaten egg whites.
Turn .... into oiled casserole.
Bake .... at 300 degrees for 45 minutes.
Yields ...... 4 servings.

Sandra Loches
Land's End, Oregon

MUSHROOM GARDEN BAKE

1 lb. fresh mushrooms, cut into halves
1 lb. cherry tomatoes
1/4 lb. zucchini, sliced 1/2 in. thick
1 tsp. each Italian seasoning, onion powder
1/4 tsp. garlic powder
1 tsp. salt
1/8 tsp. pepper
2 tbsp. olive oil
1 tbsp. melted butter

Layer ...... vegetables in baking dish.
Combine .... seasonings and sprinkle over vegetables.
Sprinkle .... with olive oil and butter.
Bake .... tightly covered, at 350 degrees for 25 minutes.
Toss .... lightly to mix before serving.
Yields ...... 6 servings.

Jewell Fields
White Oaks, Montana

OKRA CREOLE

24 young tender okra pods, sliced
1 sm. onion, minced
1 clove of garlic, minced
1/2 sm. green pepper, minced
2 tbsp. butter
2 tomatoes, coarsely chopped
Salt and pepper to taste

Saute ...... first 4 ingredients in butter in skillet for 6 minutes.
Stir .... in remaining ingredients.
Simmer ..... for 10 minutes or until okra is tender.
Yields ...... 6 servings.

Ernestine Carver
Downers Grove, Texas

BAKED ONIONS WITH MUSTARD SAUCE

6 lg. mild onions
1 c. toasted bread crumbs
6 tbsp. melted butter
2 tbsp. chopped parsley
1/4 tsp. poultry seasoning
3/4 tsp. salt
Pepper to taste
2 tbsp. flour
1 1/2 c. milk
1 tbsp. mustard
2 tbsp. lemon juice

Cook . . . . onions in boiling water to cover in saucepan for 30 minutes or until tender; cool and remove centers.
Combine . . . . crumbs with 1/4 cup butter, parsley, poultry seasoning, 1/4 teaspoon salt and dash of pepper in bowl, mixing well.
Spoon . . . . . . into onions in buttered baking dish.
Bake . . . . at 350 degrees for 30 minutes.
Blend . . . . . . 2 tablespoons butter with flour and remaining 1/2 teaspoon salt in saucepan.
Stir . . . . in milk gradually.
Cook . . . . until thick, stirring constantly.
Blend . . . . . . in mustard and lemon juice just before serving.
Spoon . . . . . . over onions.

Photograph for this recipe on this page.

HONEY-GINGER ONIONS

16 whole onions, cooked
1/4 c. honey
2 tbsp. butter
1 tbsp. paprika
1/2 tsp. salt
1/4 tsp. ginger

Arrange . . . . . onions in shallow buttered baking dish.
Blend . . . . . . remaining ingredients in saucepan.
Cook . . . . for 5 minutes.
Spoon . . . . . . over onions.
Bake . . . . at 325 degrees for 10 minutes.

Sheela Vercher
Socorro, New Mexico

CITRUS HONEY PEAS

1 1/2 tsp. each grated orange and lemon
* rind*
2 tbsp. butter
Juice of 1 orange and 1 lemon
1/4 c. honey
1   16-oz. can early garden peas, drained
1/4 c. chopped pimento

Saute . . . . . . rinds in butter in skillet.
Stir . . . . in juices and honey.
Boil . . . . until thickened.
Stir . . . . in peas and pimento.
Heat . . . . to serving temperature.
Yields . . . . . . 4 servings.

Mary Hansell
Ely, Nevada

CLASSIC FRENCH PEAS

2 lb. shelled peas
6 lettuce leaves
6 sm. onions
1/2 tsp. salt
1/4 tsp. thyme
1 tsp. sugar
1 tbsp. butter

Place . . . . peas in lettuce-lined saucepan.
Add . . . . remaining ingredients except butter with 1/4 cup water.
Simmer . . . . . covered, for 25 minutes or until tender.
Place . . . . peas and onions in serving dish.
Top . . . . with butter.
Yields . . . . . . 4 servings.

Helen Swanson
Palo Alto, California

PEAS AND ONIONS AMANDINE

1/2 c. slivered almonds
2 tbsp. melted butter
1 c. diagonally sliced celery, cooked, drained
1 sm. can whole onions
1 10-oz. package frozen English peas, cooked
Salt and pepper to taste

Saute . . . . . . almonds in butter in skillet.
Combine . . . . all ingredients in saucepan.
Heat . . . . to serving temperature.

Chandra Barstow
Couer d'Alene, Idaho

CORN-STUFFED GREEN PEPPERS

4 med. green peppers
1 1/2 c. corn
1 c. chopped tomato
1/4 c. finely chopped celery
1 tbsp. finely chopped onion
2 tbsp. melted butter
2 eggs, slightly beaten
1 1/4 tsp. salt
1/8 tsp. pepper
1/2 c. soft bread crumbs
1 tsp. sugar (opt.)

Cut . . . . tops from peppers and remove seeds.
Parboil . . . . . for 3 to 5 minutes; drain well.
Combine . . . . remaining ingredients in bowl, mixing well.
Spoon . . . . . . into peppers.
Place . . . . in greased casserole with a small amount of water.
Bake . . . . covered, at 350 degrees for 1 hour.

Mabel Carson
Sharon, Utah

SAUCY STUFFED PEPPERS

6 med. green peppers
1 1/2 c. tomato sauce
2 c. chopped fresh mushrooms
1 c. cottage cheese with chives
1/2 c. noninstant powdered skim milk
Salt to taste
1/4 tsp. pepper
1 tsp. onion juice

2 tbsp. wheat germ
1 tbsp. safflower oil
1/2 c. soy powder
1/2 c. grated Cheddar cheese

Slice . . . . tops from green peppers, removing seeds.
Place . . . . in muffin cups.
Combine . . . . 1 cup tomato sauce and remaining ingredients except Cheddar cheese in bowl, mixing well.
Spoon . . . . . . into prepared pepper cups.
Top . . . . with Cheddar cheese.
Bake . . . . at 350 degrees for 1/2 hour.
Pour . . . . remaining tomato sauce over top.
Bake . . . . for 10 minutes longer.
Yields . . . . . . 6 servings.

Amelia Eggers
Potsdale, Arizona

ALPINE POTATO CASSEROLE

4 c. cooked cubed potatoes
1 c. yogurt
1 c. low-fat cottage cheese
1/4 c. chopped chives
1 tsp. salt
Dash of garlic powder

Combine . . . . all ingredients in bowl, mixing well.
Place . . . . in nonstick baking pan.
Bake . . . . at 350 degrees for 30 minutes or until bubbly.

Connie Hightower
Phillips, Indiana

EASY-BAKED POTATOES

3 lg. baking potatoes, thickly sliced
1 tsp. each onion salt, celery salt
Dash of pepper
1/3 c. grated Parmesan cheese
1/3 c. butter

Spread . . . . . potatoes in baking dish.
Sprinkle . . . . with seasonings and cheese.
Dot . . . . with butter.
Bake . . . . covered, at 350 degrees for 30 to 45 minutes or until tender.

Ginny Elkins
Marsh Valley, Montana

CREOLE STUFFED POTATOES

1 c. chopped onions
1/2 c. chopped green pepper
2 tbsp. butter
1 c. chopped tomatoes
6 lg. baked potatoes
2 tbsp. milk
Salt and pepper to taste

Saute ...... onions and green pepper in butter in skillet.
Stir .... in tomatoes.
Cook .... for 2 minutes.
Cut .... potatoes in half lengthwise, scooping out pulp and reserving shells.
Mash .... pulp with milk and seasonings in bowl.
Fold .... in tomato mixture.
Spoon ...... into shells.
Place .... on baking sheet.
Dot .... with additional butter and garnish with paprika.
Bake .... at 400 degrees for 20 minutes.
Yields ...... 6 servings.

Wendy Marshall
Marion, Ohio

POTATO PUFF

2 c. mashed potatoes
1 tbsp. butter
1 egg, separated
1 tsp. chopped parsley

Combine .... potatoes, butter and beaten egg yolk, beating until light.
Fold .... in stiffly beaten egg white and parsley.
Pour .... into buttered baking dish.
Garnish ..... with shredded cheese.
Bake .... at 350 degrees for 30 minutes.
Yields ...... 4 servings.

Marilyn Osborne
Cutters Corner, Vermont

NEW POTATO CURRY

1 1/2 tbsp. chopped onion
2 tbsp. butter
3/4 tsp. curry powder
1 1/2 tbsp. flour
3/4 tsp. salt
1 1/2 c. skim milk
3 lb. new potatoes, cooked, peeled

Saute .... onion in butter in skillet until tender.
Blend ...... in curry powder, flour and salt.
Stir .... in milk gradually.
Cook .... until thick, stirring constantly.
Place .... potatoes in 2-quart casserole.
Top .... with sauce.
Bake .... at 375 degrees for 30 minutes or until bubbly.
Yields ...... 8 servings.

C. J. Samson
Newton, Mississippi

RUTABAGA MAGIC

1 1/2 to 2 lb. rutabagas, peeled, chopped
1 1/2 tsp. Worcestershire sauce
1/4 tsp. onion powder
1/4 c. sugar
1 tsp. salt
3 or 4 drops of Tabasco sauce
Butter to taste

Combine .... all ingredients except butter with water to cover in saucepan.
Cook .... until tender; drain.
Mash .... with butter and serve immediately.

Sally Andrews
Boston, Massachusetts

EASY SPINACH RING

3 c. drained cooked spinach
1/2 c. coarse bread crumbs
1 tsp. onion juice
1 tbsp. chopped celery
1/4 tsp. salt
1/4 tsp. pepper
2 tbsp. margarine, melted
3 eggs, beaten
Cauliflowerets, cooked
Carrots, cooked

Combine .... first 8 ingredients in bowl, mixing well.
Spoon ...... into buttered ring mold.
Place .... in pan of hot water.
Bake .... at 300 degrees for 30 minutes or until set.
Unmold .... onto serving platter.

Fill . . . . center with cauliflower and surround with carrots.

Yields . . . . . . 6 servings.

Loraine Stevenson
Paris, Kentucky

SPINACH SOUFFLE

1 tbsp. each minced onion, green pepper,
   celery
3 tbsp. margarine
3 tbsp. flour
Salt to taste
1/8 tsp. pepper
1 c. milk
4 eggs, separated
2 c. cooked spinach, drained

Saute . . . . . . first 3 vegetables in margarine in saucepan until tender.

Stir . . . . in flour, salt and pepper.

Add . . . . milk gradually, stirring constantly.

Cook . . . . until thick, stirring constantly.

Stir . . . . a small amount of hot mixture into beaten egg yolks; stir egg yolks into hot mixture.

Add . . . . spinach, mixing well.

Fold . . . . in stiffly beaten egg whites.

Spoon . . . . . . into greased 1-quart casserole.

Place . . . . in pan of hot water.

Bake . . . . at 350 degrees for 50 minutes.

Yields . . . . . . 6 servings.

Toni Guast
Factoryville, Pennsylvania

SESAME SPINACH

1/4 c. soy sauce
2 tbsp. cider vinegar
1/4 tsp. sugar
2 pkg. frozen leaf spinach, cooked, drained
1 med. onion, cut into rings
2 tbsp. toasted sesame seed

Combine . . . . first 3 ingredients in small bowl.

Toss . . . . with spinach and onion rings in large bowl.

Chill . . . . for 1 hour, tossing frequently.

Sprinkle . . . . with sesame seed before serving.

Yields . . . . . . 6-8 servings.

Roberta Jones
Cheyenne, Wyoming

GOLDEN EMERALD BAKED SQUASH

1 yellow squash, sliced
1 zucchini, sliced
2 tbsp. melted butter
1/2 c. each walnuts, Parmesan cheese
2 tbsp. chopped fresh dill

Arrange . . . . . half the squash and zucchini in shallow casserole.

Brush . . . . . . with butter.

Sprinkle . . . . mixture of walnuts, cheese and dill over vegetables.

Top . . . . with remaining vegetables.

Bake . . . . at 350 degrees for 25 to 30 minutes or until squash is tender.

Photograph for this recipe on page 85.

CRUNCHY MICROWAVE SQUASH

4 tsp. margarine
2 acorn squash, halved, seeded
4 tbsp. each brown sugar, crushed peanuts,
   coconut

Place . . . . 1 teaspoon margarine in each squash half.

Sprinkle . . . . with remaining ingredients.

Arrange . . . . . in glass baking dish.

Microwave . . on High for 5 to 6 minutes or until sugar is bubbly.

Yields . . . . . . 4 servings.

Trellis Baker
Jackson, Georgia

SQUASH CHILI VERDE

6 to 8 sm. yellow squash, sliced
1 med. onion, sliced
2 tbsp. butter
1 to 3 hot green chili peppers
Salt and pepper to taste
4 slices American cheese

Cook . . . . squash and onion in butter in covered skillet until tender, stirring several times.

Add . . . . chili peppers, salt and pepper.

Cook . . . . for 15 minutes longer.

Arrange . . . . . cheese over top.

Heat . . . . until cheese melts.

Yields . . . . . . 8 servings.

Martha Matthews
Colorado City, Texas

PARTY SQUASH RING

6 c. chopped yellow squash
1 med. onion, chopped
1/2 med. green pepper, chopped
1 clove of garlic, chopped
Salt to taste
2 tbsp. sugar
1/4 c. melted margarine
1 tbsp. Worcestershire sauce
1/2 tsp. pepper
1/2 tsp. Tabasco sauce
1 c. bread crumbs
3 eggs, well beaten
1/2 c. milk

Cook . . . . first 4 vegetables in water in saucepan until tender; drain well.
Combine . . . . remaining ingredients in bowl, mixing well.
Stir . . . . in vegetables.
Spoon . . . . . . into greased 1 1/2-quart ring mold.
Bake . . . . at 350 degrees for 40 minutes or until firm.
Unmold . . . . onto serving platter.
Fill . . . . center with cooked green peas.

Ernestine Hodson
Grand Prairie, Texas

TOMATOES SAINT GERMAIN

6 lg. tomatoes
Salt and pepper to taste
5 tsp. lemon juice
3 c. cooked English peas
3 tbsp. instant minced onion
1/2 tsp. Worcestershire sauce
3 tbsp. bread crumbs

Slice . . . . tops from tomatoes.
Remove . . . . and chop pulp; drain shells.
Sprinkle . . . . shells with salt, pepper and 3 teaspoons lemon juice.
Combine . . . . remaining 2 teaspoons lemon juice, peas, onion and Worcestershire sauce with chopped tomatoes in bowl, mixing well.
Spoon . . . . . . into tomato shells.
Top . . . . with crumbs.
Bake . . . . at 300 degrees for 15 minutes or until heated through.

Frances Jones
Littlefield, Texas

BROILED TOMATOES NAPOLI

4 lg. tomatoes, thickly sliced
1 c. fresh bread crumbs
1/4 c. melted butter
2 tbsp. grated Parmesan cheese
1/2 tsp. Italian herb seasoning

Place . . . . tomatoes in broiler pan.
Combine . . . . remaining ingredients in bowl, mixing well.
Spread . . . . . over tomatoes.
Broil . . . . 10 inches from heat source for 4 to 5 minutes or until heated through.

Barbara Hammerberg
Hortonville, Wisconsin

TOP-OF-THE-STOVE TURNIPS

3 c. thinly sliced white turnips
2 c. sliced carrots
1/2 c. sliced onion
1/4 c. diced celery
1/4 c. chopped green pepper
1 c. skim milk
1 tsp. salt
1 tbsp. margarine
1 c. grated American cheese
3 tbsp. finely crumbled crackers

Combine . . . . vegetables with milk, salt and 1 cup water in saucepan.
Simmer . . . . . covered, for 20 minutes or until tender.
Stir . . . . in remaining ingredients.
Cook . . . . covered, until cheese is melted.

Cassie Bridges
Biloxi, Mississippi

CHEESY ZUCCHINI BAKE

2 c. bread crumbs
1 clove of garlic, crushed
1 tsp. each basil, rosemary, parsley
1/2 tsp. salt
1/4 tsp. pepper
5 sm. zucchini, thinly sliced
1 c. grated Parmesan cheese

Combine . . . . bread crumbs, garlic and seasonings in bowl, mixing well.
Layer . . . . . . half the zucchini, crumb mixture and cheese in greased 9 x 9-inch baking pan.

Sprinkle . . . . with a small amount of oil.
Repeat . . . . . layers.
Bake . . . . at 375 degrees for 1 hour or until golden brown.
Yields . . . . . . 6 servings.

Deborah Block
Plymouth, Massachusetts

COLORFUL ZUCCHINI CASSEROLE

1 lb. zucchini, cubed
1 12-oz. can whole kernel corn, drained
2 med. cloves of garlic, crushed
2 tbsp. salad oil
1 tsp. salt
1/4 tsp. pepper
1/2 c. shredded mozzarella cheese

Combine . . . . first 6 ingredients in large skillet.
Cook . . . . covered, over medium heat for 10 minutes or until zucchini is tender-crisp.
Stir . . . . in cheese.
Heat . . . . to serving temperature.

Barbara Porter
Phoenix, Arizona

CURRIED ZUCCHINI

1 sm. zucchini, thinly sliced
1 sm. scallop squash, thinly sliced
2 sm. onions, sliced
1 green tomato, sliced
1/2 green pepper, diced
2 to 3 tbsp. butter
1 tsp. curry powder
1 tsp. salt

Combine . . . . all ingredients in skillet with a small amount of water.
Cook . . . . covered, over medium heat until vegetables are tender-crisp.

Marian Earnhart
McConnelsville, Ohio

ITALIAN MEDLEY

2 zucchini, thinly sliced
2 med. potatoes, thinly sliced
1/2 med. onion, sliced
2 med. tomatoes, sliced
Italian seasoning, salt and pepper to taste
Buttered bread crumbs

Layer . . . . . . vegetables in casserole, sprinkling each layer with seasonings.
Sprinkle . . . . with crumbs.
Bake . . . . at 350 degrees for 45 minutes.
Yields . . . . . . 4 servings.

April Reed
Conroy, Arkansas

RATATOUILLE

1 med. eggplant, peeled, coarsely chopped
1 med. zucchini, sliced
1 green pepper, sliced
1 onion, sliced
2 c. chopped tomatoes
1 clove of garlic, finely chopped
1/2 tsp. dried basil
Salt to taste
1/4 tsp. pepper
2 tbsp. oil

Layer . . . . . . first 5 ingredients in casserole.
Combine . . . . garlic with remaining ingredients in small bowl.
Sprinkle . . . . over vegetables.
Bake . . . . covered, at 350 degrees for 40 minutes.

Darla Long
Hamilton, Ohio

VEGETABLE SOUFFLE

2 c. milk
2 tbsp. margarine
4 slices bread, trimmed, cubed
3 eggs, beaten
2 c. cooked green beans
1 c. cooked carrots
1 c. cooked peas
1 onion, chopped
1/2 c. grated Tillamook cheese

Scald . . . . milk with margarine in saucepan.
Stir . . . . in bread; remove from heat.
Add . . . . eggs, mixing well.
Arrange . . . . . vegetables in greased baking dish.
Pour . . . . milk mixture over top.
Top . . . . with cheese.
Bake . . . . at 325 degrees for 45 minutes.
Yields . . . . . . 4 servings.

Doris Waller
Chino, California

HERB GRILLED VEGETABLES

1/2 c. margarine, melted
1 tbsp. each onion powder, parsley flakes
1 tsp. each basil, garlic powder
1/2 tsp. salt
1/8 tsp. pepper
2 med. zucchini, halved lengthwise
1 med. eggplant, cut in 1/2-in. slices
2 med. tomatoes, halved crosswise

Blend ...... margarine with seasonings in small bowl.
Brush ...... over vegetables.
Grill .... zucchini and eggplant over hot coals for 5 minutes; turn.
Place .... tomatoes cut side up on grill.
Cook .... for 5 minutes longer, basting occasionally.

Sophie Passman
Danville, Illinois

LAYERED VEGETABLE CASSEROLE

1 lb. mushrooms, sliced
1 tbsp. butter
3 med. yellow squash, sliced, cooked, drained
2 lg. slices mozzarella cheese
10 oz. spinach, cooked, drained
1/4 c. grated Parmesan cheese

Saute ...... mushrooms in butter in skillet.
Layer ...... squash, 1 slice mozzarella, mushrooms, remaining slice mozzarella and spinach in casserole.
Top .... with Parmesan cheese.
Bake .... at 400 degrees for 20 minutes or until bubbly.

Lillian Cleveland
Fallon, Nevada

STIR-FRY SUMMER VEGETABLES

2 tbsp. margarine
2 tbsp. oil
2 chicken bouillon cubes
1 med. clove of garlic, minced
1 lb. zucchini, thinly sliced
1/2 lb. fresh mushrooms, sliced
4 green onions, coarsely chopped
1 sm. red or green pepper, coarsely chopped
Grated juice and rind of 1/2 lemon

Combine .... first 4 ingredients in large skillet, stirring until bouillon dissolves.
Add .... zucchini and mushrooms to hot mixture.
Stir-fry ..... over medium-high heat for 3 minutes.
Add .... onions and pepper.
Stir-fry ..... for 2 minutes longer.
Stir .... in lemon juice and rind.
Serve .... immediately.
Yields ...... 6 servings.

Roberta Gray
Tampa, Florida

SPRINGTIME MEDLEY

1 bunch broccoli, cut into bite-sized pieces
2 sm. zucchini, sliced
1/2 lb. asparagus, sliced
1 lg. clove of garlic, chopped
1 basket cherry tomatoes, cut into halves
1 tsp. basil
1/2 lb. mushrooms, thinly sliced
1/2 c. frozen peas
1/4 c. chopped parsley
Salt to taste
1/2 tsp. pepper
1/4 c. melted margarine
3/4 c. evaporated skim milk
2/3 c. Parmesan cheese
1 lb. thin spaghetti, cooked, drained

Cook .... first 3 ingredients in a small amount of water until tender-crisp; drain.
Stir-fry ..... garlic and tomatoes in a small amount of oil in large skillet for 2 minutes.
Add .... basil and mushrooms.
Stir-fry ..... for 3 minutes.
Add .... next 4 ingredients.
Cook .... for 1 minute longer.
Combine .... stir-fried mixture with broccoli mixture.
Heat .... margarine, milk and cheese in skillet, stirring until smooth.
Add .... spaghetti, stirring until coated.
Stir .... in vegetable mixture.
Heat .... to serving temperature.
Yields ...... 8 servings.

Ashley Bruna
Metro City, Oklahoma

breads

CHEESY APPLESAUCE BISCUITS

3 tbsp. shortening
2 c. self-rising flour, sifted
1 3-oz. package cream cheese, softened
1 c. grated sharp cheese
1 c. applesauce
2 eggs, slightly beaten

Cut . . . . shortening into flour in large bowl until crumbly.
Combine . . . . remaining ingredients in bowl, mixing well.
Add . . . . to flour mixture, mixing well.
Knead . . . . . . on lightly floured surface.
Roll . . . . and cut with biscuit cutter.
Place . . . . on greased baking sheet.
Bake . . . . at 375 degrees for 10 to 12 minutes or until brown.
Yields . . . . . . 20-25 servings.

Lunette Larson
Jasmine, Florida

WHOLE WHEAT BISCUITS

2 c. whole wheat flour
4 tsp. baking powder
1/2 tsp. salt
4 tbsp. shortening
1 c. milk

Sift . . . . first 3 ingredients together into bowl, adding any bran remaining in sifter.
Cut . . . . in shortening until crumbly.
Add . . . . milk, mixing well.
Drop . . . . by spoonfuls onto greased baking sheet.
Bake . . . . at 425 degrees for 12 minutes.
Yields . . . . . . 16 servings.

Lenette Charles
Westland, Vermont

BRAN CORN BREAD

1/2 c. sugar
1/2 c. shortening
2 eggs, beaten
1 1/2 c. All-Bran
1 c. milk
1 c. flour
1/2 c. yellow cornmeal
3 tsp. baking powder
1/2 tsp. salt

Cream . . . . . . sugar and shortening in bowl.
Add . . . . eggs, mixing well.
Stir . . . . in All-Bran and milk.
Let . . . . stand for 5 minutes or longer.
Add . . . . sifted dry ingredients, mixing well.
Pour . . . . into greased 9 x 13-inch baking pan.
Bake . . . . at 375 degrees until bread tests done.
Yields . . . . . . 8 servings.

Ada Westmoreland
Leach, Virginia

FLAT BREAD

1/2 c. sugar
1/2 c. oil
4 c. buttermilk
3 c. all-purpose flour
2 tsp. baking powder
2 tsp. soda
3 c. whole wheat flour
1 tsp. salt

Blend . . . . . . sugar and oil in bowl.
Stir . . . . in buttermilk gradually.
Sift . . . . next 3 dry ingredients together.
Add . . . . to buttermilk mixture with whole wheat flour mixed with salt, mixing well.
Divide . . . . . . into equal portions of desired size.
Roll . . . . very thin on floured surface.
Place . . . . on baking sheets.
Bake . . . . at 375 degrees for 12 minutes or until brown and crisp.

Ruth Radcliffe
Billings, Montana

BANANA-BRAN BREAD

1/3 c. shortening
3/4 c. sugar
1 egg, well beaten
2 c. bran flakes
1 1/2 c. mashed bananas
1 1/2 c. sifted flour
2 tsp. baking powder
1/2 tsp. each soda, salt
1/2 c. chopped walnuts
1 tsp. vanilla extract

Cream . . . . . . shortening and sugar in bowl.
Mix . . . . in egg and bran flakes.

Add .... bananas mixed with 2 table-spoons water alternately with sifted dry ingredients, mixing well after each addition.
Stir .... in walnuts and vanilla.
Pour .... into large greased loaf pan.
Bake .... at 350 degrees for 1 hour or until loaf tests done.

Irene Castle
Bradley's Fork, Utah

BARLEY-WHEAT BREAD

2 c. barley flour
2 c. whole wheat flour
1 c. packed brown sugar
4 tsp. baking powder
1 1/2 tsp. soda
1/2 tsp. salt
1 1/2 c. milk
4 eggs, slightly beaten

Combine .... first 6 ingredients in bowl, mixing well.
Add .... remaining ingredients, mixing well.
Place .... in 2 greased loaf pans.
Bake .... at 350 degrees for 30 to 40 minutes or until loaves test done.

Annie Holbrook
Pascagoula, Mississippi

BROWN BREAD

2 c. flour
1/2 tsp. salt
1 1/2 c. sugar
2 tsp. soda
3 c. All-Bran
1 c. whole wheat flour
3 tbsp. molasses
3 c. buttermilk
1 c. chopped nuts

Combine .... first 6 ingredients in bowl, mixing well.
Add .... molasses and buttermilk, mixing well.
Stir .... in nuts.
Place .... in 2 greased loaf pans.
Bake .... at 325 degrees for 1 1/2 hours or until bread tests done.

Rose Denney
Yokum, Arkansas

BLUEBERRY GINGERBREAD

1/2 c. shortening
1 c. sugar
1 egg, beaten
1 tsp. soda
1 c. buttermilk
2 c. flour
1/2 tsp. ginger
1 tsp. cinnamon
1/2 tsp. salt
3 tbsp. molasses
1 c. fresh blueberries

Combine .... first 3 ingredients in bowl, mixing well.
Dissolve .... soda in buttermilk.
Add .... to creamed mixture alternately with combined dry ingredients, mixing well after each addition.
Fold .... in molasses and blueberries.
Pour .... into 8-inch square pan.
Bake .... at 350 degrees for 30 to 35 minutes.

Sue Belcher
Tampa, Florida

 Bake corn bread batter in waffle iron for reduced portions — new texture treat too.

BUTTERMILK-RAISIN BREAD

5 c. sifted flour
1 c. sugar
1 tbsp. baking powder
1 1/2 tsp. salt
1 tsp. soda
1/2 c. butter
2 1/2 c. white seedless raisins
3 tbsp. caraway seed
2 1/2 c. buttermilk
1 egg, slightly beaten

Sift .... first 5 ingredients into bowl.
Cut .... in butter until crumbly.
Mix .... in raisins and caraway seed.
Add .... buttermilk and egg, stirring until just moistened.
Pour .... into buttered casserole.
Bake .... at 350 degrees for 1 hour or until loaf tests done.

Beulah Wilson
Seattle, Washington

CARROT BREAD

3 eggs
1 1/2 c. oil
2 c. sugar
2 c. grated carrots
1 sm. can crushed pineapple
1 c. chopped walnuts
3 tsp. vanilla extract
3 c. flour
1/2 tsp. salt
1 tsp. soda
2 tbsp. cinnamon

Combine .... first 3 ingredients in bowl, beating well.
Add .... carrots, pineapple, walnuts and vanilla, mixing well.
Beat .... in remaining dry ingredients.
Pour .... into 2 greased loaf pans.
Bake .... at 325 degrees for 1 hour.

Veda Prince
Glascow, Montana

GRAHAM BREAD

1 c. all-purpose flour
2 c. graham flour
1 tsp. salt
1/2 c. packed brown sugar
1 1/2 tsp. soda
2 c. buttermilk

Combine .... first 4 ingredients in bowl.
Stir .... soda into buttermilk.
Add .... to dry ingredients, mixing well.
Pour .... into greased loaf pan.
Bake .... at 350 degrees for 1 hour or until loaf tests done.

Starr Winslow
Carson City, Nevada

GRAPE NUTS BREAD

1 c. Grape Nuts
2 c. buttermilk
1 tbsp. melted shortening
1 c. sugar
2 eggs, beaten
4 c. flour
2 tsp. baking powder
1 tsp. soda

Combine .... Grape Nuts with buttermilk in bowl.
Let .... stand until soft.
Add .... remaining ingredients, mixing well.
Pour .... into loaf pan.
Bake .... at 350 degrees for 1 hour or until bread tests done.

Erna Watkins
Glen Elden, California

SPICY HEALTH BREAD

1/2 c. shortening
1/2 c. packed brown sugar
1/2 c. honey
2 eggs
1 c. cottage cheese
1/4 c. unsweetened apple butter
1/2 tsp. ginger
1/4 tsp. cinnamon
1/4 tsp. salt
3/4 tsp. soda
2 c. flour
2 tsp. baking powder
1/2 c. raisins

Combine .... first 3 ingredients in bowl, beating until creamy.
Beat .... in eggs, cottage cheese and apple butter.
Add .... remaining ingredients except raisins, mixing until smooth.
Stir .... in raisins.
Pour .... into greased casserole.
Bake .... at 375 degrees for 45 minutes or until loaf tests done.

Mary Nell Miller
Bowker, Arizona

MARMALADE PAN BREAD

1 c. whole bran cereal
3/4 c. milk
1 egg
1/4 c. shortening
1 c. sifted flour
2 1/2 tsp. baking powder
1/2 tsp. salt
1/4 c. sugar
1/2 c. orange marmalade

Combine . . . . cereal with milk in bowl.
Let . . . . stand until milk is absorbed.
Add . . . . egg and shortening, beating well.
Sift . . . . flour, baking powder, salt and sugar together.
Add . . . . to cereal mixture, stirring until just mixed.
Spread . . . . . in greased 9 x 9-inch baking pan.
Place . . . . spoonfuls of marmalade on top, pressing lightly into dough.
Bake . . . . at 400 degrees for 25 minutes or until lightly browned.

Photograph for this recipe above.

OATMEAL-APPLESAUCE BREAD

1 1/2 c. rolled oats
1/2 c. all-purpose flour
1/2 c. whole wheat flour
1/2 c. packed brown sugar
1/4 c. bran
1 tsp. each soda, baking powder
1 tsp. cinnamon
1/2 tsp. salt
1 c. applesauce
1/3 c. oil
2 eggs
1 c. raisins
1/2 c. chopped black walnuts

Combine . . . . first 9 ingredients in bowl.
Add . . . . remaining ingredients except raisins and walnuts, mixing well.
Stir . . . . in raisins and walnuts.
Pour . . . . into greased and floured loaf pan.
Bake . . . . at 350 degrees for 50 to 60 minutes or until loaf tests done.
Cool . . . . for 10 minutes before removing from pan.

Lois Allison
Dryden, Kentucky

PRUNE-OAT BREAD

2 c. sifted flour
2 1/2 tsp. baking powder
1/2 tsp. soda
1 1/4 tsp. salt
1/2 c. sugar
1 c. rolled oats
2 tbsp. melted shortening
1 1/4 c. buttermilk
1 c. drained cooked prunes, finely chopped
1/2 c. chopped nuts

Combine . . . . first 6 ingredients in bowl.
Add . . . . shortening and buttermilk, stirring until just moistened.
Stir . . . . in prunes and nuts.
Pour . . . . into greased loaf pan.
Bake . . . . at 350 degrees for 50 minutes or until loaf tests done.

Regena Polk
Rogers, Oklahoma

PINEAPPLE-BRAN MUFFINS

2 eggs, beaten
1 tsp. baking powder
1 tsp. cinnamon
1 tsp. vanilla extract
2/3 c. nonfat dry milk
2 tbsp. sugar
2/3 c. All-Bran
1/4 c. crushed pineapple

Combine . . . . first 6 ingredients in bowl, mixing well.
Stir . . . . in remaining ingredients.
Spoon . . . . . . into 6 greased muffin cups.
Bake . . . . at 350 degrees for 15 minutes.

Ruth Sanborn
Pekin, Illinois

RAISIN-RYE MUFFINS

1 c. flour
1 c. rye flour
2 tbsp. sugar
3 tsp. baking powder
1/2 tsp. salt
1/2 c. raisins
1 c. milk
2 tbsp. molasses
1/4 c. oil
2 eggs, beaten

Sift .... first 5 dry ingredients into bowl.
Stir .... in raisins.
Combine .... remaining ingredients in small bowl.
Add .... to dry ingredients, stirring until just moistened.
Fill .... greased muffin cups 2/3 full.
Bake .... at 400 degrees for 20 to 25 minutes.

Junelaine Richards
Washington Valley, New Jersey

ROLLED OATS MUFFINS

1 c. rolled oats
1/3 c. sugar
1 c. flour
1 tsp. (scant) soda
1/4 c. shortening, melted
1 c. buttermilk
1 egg

Combine .... first 4 ingredients in bowl.
Add .... remaining ingredients, mixing well.
Spoon ...... into greased muffin cups.
Bake .... at 350 degrees for 20 minutes or until brown.

Clarice Fullman
Franklin, Maine

OATMEAL PANCAKES

2 c. oats
2 3/4 c. buttermilk
1 1/2 c. flour
2 tbsp. sugar
1 tsp. each baking powder, salt
1 tsp. soda
2 eggs, slightly beaten
2 tbsp. melted butter

1   12-oz. jar Welch's grape jam
2 tbsp. orange juice
1 tsp. grated orange rind
Dash of allspice

Combine .... oats and buttermilk in bowl, mixing well.
Let .... stand overnight.
Sift .... flour, sugar, baking powder and salt into bowl.
Add .... oat mixture, soda dissolved in 2 tablespoons water, eggs and butter.
Beat .... until smooth.
Bake .... 1/4 cup at a time on lightly greased hot griddle, turning once.
Combine .... remaining ingredients in saucepan.
Heat .... to serving temperature, stirring constantly.
Serve .... over pancakes.
Yields ...... 16 pancakes.

Photograph for this recipe above.

BRAN PANCAKES

1 1/2 c. 100% bran cereal
1 1/2 c. flour
4 tsp. baking powder

1 tsp. each salt, sugar
1 tbsp. melted butter
2 1/2 c. milk
1 egg, separated

Combine .... first 5 ingredients in mixer bowl.
Add .... butter, milk and egg yolk, beating well.
Fold .... in stiffly beaten egg white.
Bake .... on hot greased griddle.
Yields ...... 6 servings.

Patsy Thornton
Eaglesville, New York

BANANA WAFFLES

2 c. flour
3 tsp. baking powder
1/4 tsp. salt
1/2 tsp. grated lemon rind (opt.)
3 eggs, separated
1 1/4 c. milk
5 tbsp. margarine
1 c. mashed ripe banana
1 tbsp. cornstarch
1/4 tsp. salt
1 1/2 c. apricot nectar
2 tbsp. honey
1 tbsp. lemon juice
3 bananas, sliced

Combine .... first 4 ingredients in large bowl.
Beat .... egg yolks with milk, 3 tablespoons melted margarine and banana until smooth.
Add .... to flour mixture, stirring until just moistened.
Fold .... in stiffly beaten egg whites.
Let .... stand for 5 to 10 minutes.
Bake .... in hot waffle iron.
Blend ...... cornstarch and salt with a small amount of nectar in saucepan.
Stir .... in remaining nectar and honey gradually.
Cook .... over low heat until thick, stirring constantly; remove from heat.
Add .... lemon juice and remaining 2 tablespoons margarine, stirring until margarine melts.
Stir .... in sliced bananas.
Serve .... over waffles.

Laurie Linville
Durham, North Carolina

RANCHERO RAISED BISCUITS

2/3 c. dark seedless raisins
1 c. milk, scalded
2 tbsp. sugar
3 tbsp. shortening
1 1/2 tsp. salt
Yellow cornmeal
1 pkg. yeast
1 egg, beaten
2 1/2 c. sifted flour
Butter, melted

Combine .... first 5 ingredients and 1/2 cup cornmeal in bowl, mixing well.
Dissolve .... yeast in 3 tablespoons warm water in warm bowl.
Add .... to raisin mixture with egg and flour, mixing well.
Drop .... by spoonfuls into 9-inch round baking pan sprinkled with cornmeal.
Brush ...... with butter and sprinkle with cornmeal.
Let .... rise in warm place for about 45 minutes or until doubled in bulk.
Bake .... at 400 degrees for 20 minutes.

Mary Ann Mosely
Bowling Green, Kentucky

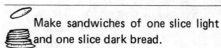 Make sandwiches of one slice light and one slice dark bread.

ANADAMA BREAD

3/4 c. yellow cornmeal
3 c. milk, scalded
3/4 c. molasses
2 tbsp. butter
2 tsp. salt
2 pkg. yeast
8 c. flour

Combine .... cornmeal, milk and 3/4 cup water in bowl, mixing well.
Stir .... in molasses, butter and salt; cool to lukewarm.
Add .... yeast and flour, mixing well.
Let .... rise until doubled in bulk.
Place .... in 2 greased loaf pans.
Bake .... at 350 degrees for 1 hour.

Hattie Burns
Steele Creek, Idaho

OATMEAL-MOLASSES LOAVES

1 pkg. dry yeast
1/4 c. light molasses
4 to 4 1/2 c. flour
1 1/2 c. oatmeal
2 eggs
2 tbsp. margarine
1 tsp. salt
1 tbsp. milk

Dissolve .... yeast in 1 3/4 cups warm water in bowl.
Stir .... in molasses.
Mix .... 2 cups flour with oatmeal, 1 egg, margarine and salt in large bowl.
Add .... dissolved yeast and enough remaining flour to make soft dough.
Knead ...... on floured surface for 8 to 10 minutes or until smooth and elastic.
Place .... in greased bowl.
Let .... rise, covered, in warm place for 1 to 1 1/2 hours or until doubled in bulk.
Shape ...... into 4 loaves.
Place .... in greased loaf pans.
Brush ...... with mixture of milk and remaining egg.
Let .... rise until doubled in bulk.
Bake .... at 400 degrees for 20 minutes or until bread tests done.

Agnes Greene
Hampton, Virginia

ONE-BOWL SALT-FREE WHITE BREAD

2 3/4 to 3 1/4 c. sifted flour
1 tbsp. sugar
1 pkg. dry yeast
2 tbsp. peanut oil

Mix .... 1 cup flour, sugar and yeast in large mixer bowl.
Stir .... in 1 cup hot water and oil.
Beat .... at medium speed for 2 minutes, scraping bowl occasionally.
Add .... 1 1/4 cups flour.
Beat .... at high speed for 2 minutes.
Stir .... in enough flour to make soft dough.
Knead ...... on floured surface until smooth and elastic.

Place .... in greased bowl, turning to coat surface.
Let .... rise, covered, until doubled in bulk.
Punch ...... dough down and shape into loaf.
Place .... in greased loaf pan.
Let .... rise, covered, until doubled in bulk.
Bake .... at 400 degrees for 30 minutes or until loaf tests done.

Dodie Hicks
Yuma, Arizona

CASSEROLE RYE BATTER BREAD

1 c. milk, scalded
3 tbsp. sugar
1 tbsp. salt
1 1/2 tbsp. shortening
2 pkg. yeast
3 c. sifted flour
1 1/2 c. unsifted rye flour
2 tsp. caraway seed

Combine .... first 4 ingredients in large bowl; cool to lukewarm.
Dissolve .... yeast in 1 cup warm water.
Add .... to milk mixture with flours and half the caraway seed, mixing well.
Let .... rise, covered, in warm place for 50 minutes or until doubled in bulk.
Stir .... batter down.
Turn .... into well-greased 1 1/2-quart casserole.
Brush ...... with additional milk.
Sprinkle .... with remaining caraway seed.
Bake .... at 400 degrees for 50 minutes.

Cassie Forman
Colorado Springs, Colorado

THREE-GRAIN BREAD

2 pkg. yeast
4 c. warm potato water
1/4 c. molasses
2 tsp. salt
3 tbsp. oil
1 c. rye flour
1 c. cornmeal
3 c. (or more) flour

Dissolve .... yeast in potato water in bowl.
Stir .... in molasses, salt and oil.
Add .... rye flour and cornmeal, mixing well.
Stir .... in enough all-purpose flour to make stiff dough.
Knead ...... on floured surface until smooth and elastic.
Divide ...... into 2 portions.
Let .... rest for 15 minutes.
Shape ...... into loaves.
Place .... in greased loaf pans.
Let .... rise in warm place until doubled in bulk.
Bake .... at 350 degrees for 40 minutes.

Violet Mansfield
South Bay, Oregon

ROUND RICE LOAVES

2 1/2 c. all-purpose flour
2 c. brown rice flour
1 1/2 c. gluten flour
1/3 c. packed brown sugar
2 tsp. salt
2 pkg. Fleischmann's Active Dry Yeast
1 1/2 c. milk
1/4 c. Fleischmann's Margarine
Cornmeal
1 egg white
Sesame seed

Combine .... flours in bowl, mixing well.
Mix .... 2 cups flour mixture and next 3 ingredients in large mixer bowl.
Combine .... milk, 1/2 cup water and margarine in saucepan.
Heat .... until very warm, 120 to 130 degrees.
Add ...... hot milk to dry ingredients gradually, beating at medium speed of electric mixer for 2 minutes, scraping bowl occasionally.
Add .... 3/4 cup flour mixture, beating at high speed for 2 minutes.
Stir .... in enough flour mixture to make stiff dough, adding additional all-purpose flour if necessary.
Knead ...... on floured surface until smooth and elastic, about 8 to 10 minutes.
Place .... in greased bowl, turning to grease surface.

Let .... rise, covered, in warm place until doubled in bulk, about 1 hour.
Punch ...... dough down, dividing in half.
Shape ...... into balls, placing on greased cornmeal sprinkled baking sheet.
Let .... rise, covered, in warm place until doubled in bulk, about 50 minutes.
Beat .... egg white with 2 tablespoons water.
Brush ...... bread with egg mixture; sprinkle with sesame seed.
Bake .... at 350 degrees for 35 minutes or until lightly browned.

Photograph for this recipe on page 97.

HONEY-ENRICHED WHOLE WHEAT BREAD

1 tbsp. yeast
2 tbsp. salt
2 tbsp. sugar
4 c. whole wheat flour
4 c. unbleached flour
1/4 c. shortening
1/2 c. honey

Dissolve .... yeast in 2 cups warm water in large mixer bowl.
Add .... salt, sugar, 1 cup whole wheat flour and 3 cups unbleached flour.
Beat .... until smooth.
Let .... rise, covered, in warm place for 1 hour.
Combine .... shortening and honey with 1 cup boiling water in bowl; cool to lukewarm.
Stir .... batter down.
Add .... remaining flours and honey mixture, beating thoroughly.
Knead ...... on floured surface for 6 to 8 minutes or until smooth and elastic.
Place .... in greased bowl, turning to grease surface.
Let .... rise, covered, for 2 hours.
Shape ...... into 3 loaves on floured surface.
Place .... in greased loaf pans.
Let .... rise, covered, for 1 hour.
Bake .... at 375 degrees for 50 minutes.

Millicent Burdett
Conklin, New Jersey

GOLDEN NUGGET BATTER MUFFINS

1 c. milk, scalded
2 c. cooked squash
1/2 c. sugar
1 pkg. yeast
2 tbsp. oil
3 c. flour
1/2 tsp. salt
1/2 tsp. soda
1/2 c. cornmeal

Combine .... first 3 ingredients in bowl; cool to lukewarm.
Dissolve .... yeast in 1/4 cup lukewarm water.
Add .... to squash mixture with oil, mixing well.
Combine .... remaining dry ingredients.
Add .... to squash mixture.
Beat .... for 3 minutes.
Let .... rise in warm place until doubled in bulk.
Fill .... muffin cups 2/3 full.
Let .... rise until doubled in bulk.
Bake .... at 375 degrees for 15 minutes.

Fay Grange
Winston-Salem, North Carolina

CARAWAY-RYE PAN ROLLS

4 c. flour
1 c. rye flour
1 tbsp. each sugar, salt
1 tbsp. caraway seed
1 pkg. dry yeast
1 c. milk
2 tbsp. honey
1 tbsp. margarine
1 egg white

Mix .... flours together.
Combine .... 1 2/3 cups flour mixture with next 4 ingredients in large bowl.
Heat .... milk, honey, margarine and 3/4 cup water to lukewarm in saucepan.
Stir .... into yeast mixture gradually.
Beat .... at medium speed for 2 minutes, scraping bowl occasionally.
Add .... 1 cup flour mixture.
Beat .... at high speed for 2 minutes.

Stir .... in enough remaining flour mixture to make soft dough.
Knead ...... on floured surface until smooth and elastic.
Place .... in greased bowl, turning to coat surface.
Let .... rise, covered, until doubled in bulk.
Punch ...... dough down.
Divide ...... in half on floured surface.
Let .... rest, covered, for 10 minutes.
Shape ...... each portion into 12 balls.
Place .... in 2 greased 9-inch cake pans.
Let .... rise, covered, until doubled in bulk.
Beat .... egg white with 2 tablespoons water.
Brush ...... over rolls.
Bake .... at 400 degrees for 25 minutes.
Cook .... on wire rack.

Debbie Taylor
Ortonville, Minnesota

SAVE-A-DAY ROLLS

1 c. shortening
3/4 c. sugar
2 tsp. salt
2 c. All-Bran
2 pkg. yeast
2 eggs, well beaten
6 c. sifted all-purpose flour

Combine .... first 4 ingredients in bowl.
Add .... 2 cups boiling water, stirring until shortening melts; cool to lukewarm.
Stir .... in yeast until dissolved.
Add .... eggs, mixing well.
Beat .... in half the flour until smooth.
Add .... remaining flour, beating until well blended.
Chill .... tightly covered, for several hours.
Punch ...... dough down.
Shape ...... into rolls.
Place .... in greased baking pan.
Let .... rise in warm place for 2 to 3 hours or until doubled in bulk.
Bake .... at 425 degrees for 12 to 14 minutes or until rolls test done.
Yields ...... 3 dozen.

Maxine Blum
White Creek, Washington

desserts

ALMOND-APPLE CAKE

1/2 c. self-rising flour
1/4 c. whole wheat flour
1 tbsp. ground almonds
1/4 c. sugar
1/2 c. butter
1 egg, lightly beaten
1/4 tsp. almond extract
4 apples, peeled and sliced
1 tbsp. raisins
1/4 c. sliced almonds
1 tbsp. confectioners' sugar

Combine .... first 5 ingredients in bowl.
Blend ...... with pastry blender.
Add .... next 2 ingredients, mixing well.
Press .... half the mixture into greased 8-inch pan.
Layer ...... with apple slices, raisins and half the sliced almonds.
Cover ...... with remaining pastry mixture.
Sprinkle .... with remaining almonds.
Bake .... at 375 degrees for 40 minutes or until apples are tender.
Garnish ..... with confectioners' sugar.

Mrs. Julie Challinger
Colorado Springs, Colorado

EGGLESS-MILKLESS-BUTTERLESS CAKE

2 c. brown sugar
4 tbsp. margarine
1 1/2 to 2 c. raisins
2 tsp. each cinnamon, cloves
2 tsp. soda
3 c. flour
1 c. chopped nuts

Combine .... first 3 ingredients, spices and 2 cups hot water in saucepan, mixing well.
Boil .... for 5 minutes; cool.
Stir .... in soda dissolved in 1 tablespoon lukewarm water.
Add .... remaining ingredients, mixing well.
Pour .... into greased and floured tube pan.
Bake .... at 350 degrees for 1 hour or until cake tests done.

Rosemary Mincks
Huntington, West Virginia

PINEAPPLE-CARROT CAKE

2 eggs
1/2 c. grated carrots
Artificial sweetener to equal
    6 tsp. sugar
3 tbsp. hominy grits
1/3 c. nonfat dry milk
2 slices unsweetened pineapple
2 tbsp. pineapple juice
1 tsp. vanilla extract
1 tsp. chopped black walnuts
1/2 tsp. coconut extract
1/4 tsp. soda

Combine .... all ingredients in blender container.
Process ..... until smooth.
Pour .... into ungreased pie plate.
Bake .... at 375 degrees for 25 minutes.

Christie Kaufman
Sheridan, Wyoming

STRAWBERRY CAKE ROLL

4 eggs
1 tsp. vanilla extract
1/2 c. sugar
3/4 c. sifted cake flour
3/4 tsp. baking powder
1/4 tsp. salt
1 tbsp. sifted confectioners' sugar
1 4-serving env. low-calorie strawberry gelatin
1 10-oz. package frozen strawberries
1 env. low-calorie dessert topping mix, prepared

Beat .... eggs and vanilla in bowl until thick and lemon colored.
Add .... sugar gradually, beating constantly.
Sift .... in next 3 dry ingredients, folding to mix.
Spread ..... in waxed paper-lined jelly roll pan.
Bake .... at 400 degrees for 10 to 12 minutes or until lightly browned.
Turn .... onto towel, sprinkled with confectioners' sugar.
Roll .... as for jelly roll.
Chill .... for several minutes.
Dissolve .... gelatin in 1 cup boiling water.
Stir .... in strawberries until thawed.

Chill . . . . until partially set.
Unroll . . . . . . cake and spread with gelatin mixture.
Chill . . . . for 10 minutes.
Roll . . . . as for jelly roll.
Chill . . . . . . for several hours.
Frost . . . . . . with whipped topping.
Chill . . . . until serving time.

Loretta Mills
State Line, Nevada

ZUCCHINI CAKE WITH CREAM CHEESE FROSTING

1 1/2 c. flour
1/2 tsp. salt
1/2 tsp. soda
1/4 tsp. baking powder
2 tsp. ground cinnamon
1 1/2 c. grated zucchini, packed
2 eggs, well beaten
1 c. fructose
1/2 c. oil
1/2 tsp. vanilla extract
1/2 c. broken walnuts
1 recipe Cream Cheese Frosting

Combine . . . . first 5 ingredients in bowl.
Combine . . . . remaining ingredients except walnuts and frosting in large bowl.
Beat . . . . in dry ingredients gradually, mixing well.
Stir . . . . in walnuts.
Pour . . . . into 2 greased and floured 9-inch cake pans.
Bake . . . . at 350 degrees for 1/2 hour or until cake tests done.
Cool . . . . and frost with Cream Cheese Frosting.

Cream Cheese Frosting

1 8-oz. package cream cheese, softened
1 stick butter, softened
1/2 c. fructose
1 tsp. vanilla extract

Combine all ingredients in mixer bowl. Beat with electric mixer until smooth.

Photograph for this recipe on page 107.

FRUIT BALLS

1/2 lb. dried apricots
1/2 lb. dried prunes
2 slices candied pineapple
1/4 lb. candied cherries
1 c. nuts
1 c. honey
3/4 c. confectioners' sugar

Force . . . . . . fruits and nuts through food grinder twice, using fine cutter.
Add . . . . honey to fruit mixture in bowl, mixing well.
Shape . . . . . . into balls.
Roll . . . . in confectioners' sugar.
Store . . . . in covered container in cool place.
Yields . . . . . . 1 1/2 pounds.

Marilyn Gornto
Perry, Georgia

HIGH-PROTEIN CHEESECAKE

8 eggs
2 c. cottage cheese
1 8-oz. package cream cheese, softened
1/2 c. sugar
3 tbsp. cornstarch
1 tsp. vanilla extract
1 tsp. rum
1 tsp. Brandy

Separate . . . . eggs, using only 1/2 cup egg yolks and reserving whites.
Place . . . . 1/2 cup egg yolks with cottage cheese in blender container.
Process . . . . . until smooth.
Add . . . . remaining ingredients except egg whites.
Process . . . . . until well blended.
Fold . . . . mixture into stiffly beaten egg whites.
Pour . . . . into 10-inch springform pan.
Place . . . . on center rack of oven.
Bake . . . . at 300 degrees for 1 hour.
Turn . . . . off oven; let stand in closed oven for 1 hour.
Yields . . . . . . 12 servings.

Mrs. Sharon K. Fox
Valparaiso, Florida

CALORIE COUNTERS' BAVARIAN

1 env. gelatin
1/3 c. cold coffee
1   10-oz. can milk chocolate Sego
1/2 tsp. rum flavoring

Soften . . . . . . gelatin in cold coffee in saucepan.
Stir . . . . in 1/2 can Sego and flavoring.
Simmer . . . . . until gelatin dissolves.
Chill . . . . in small mixer bowl until partially congealed.
Beat . . . . with electric mixer at low speed until well mixed.
Beat . . . . in remaining Sego at high speed.
Spoon . . . . . . into mold.
Chill . . . . until set.
Unmold . . . . onto serving plate.

Photograph for this recipe above.

CHOCOLATE BAVARIAN

1 env. gelatin
1/4 c. cocoa
1 c. skim milk
2 tsp. artificial sweetener
1/2 tsp. vanilla extract
1 c. nonfat dry milk

Soften . . . . . . gelatin in 2 tablespoons water.
Combine . . . . cocoa and skim milk in small saucepan, stirring until smooth.
Add . . . . gelatin and sweetener.
Simmer . . . . . until gelatin dissolves, stirring constantly.
Stir . . . . in vanilla.
Chill . . . . until partially set.
Combine . . . . dry milk powder with 1 cup ice water in mixer bowl.
Beat . . . . with electric mixer at high speed until stiff.
Add . . . . chocolate mixture gradually, beating constantly.
Spoon . . . . . . into greased mold.
Chill . . . . until firm.
Unmold . . . . onto serving plate.

Naomi Austin
Gainesville, Texas

Cook with powdered milk.

STRAWBERRY SPONGE

2 eggs, separated
1/4 tsp. salt
1 env. gelatin
4 tbsp. sugar
1   10-oz. package frozen strawberries, thawed
1 tbsp. lemon juice
1 tsp grated lemon rind

Beat . . . . egg yolks with 1/2 cup water until foamy.
Combine . . . . with salt, gelatin and 2 table-spoons sugar in top of double boiler.
Cook . . . . over boiling water until gelatin dissolves, stirring constantly.
Stir . . . . in strawberries, lemon juice and rind.
Chill . . . . until partially set.
Beat . . . . until strawberries are blended.
Beat . . . . egg whites with 2 tablespoons sugar until stiff.
Fold . . . . into strawberry mixture.
Spoon . . . . . . into mold.
Chill . . . . until set.
Unmold . . . . onto serving dish.

Gerry White
Spary, Connecticut

CAROB CHIP-OATMEAL DROPS

1 c. butter, softened
1 c. honey
2 eggs
2 tsp. vanilla extract
2 c. whole wheat flour
1/4 tsp. salt
1 tsp. soda
2 c. oats
1 c. carob chips
1/2 c. chopped nuts
1/2 c. raisins

Cream ...... butter in bowl until fluffy.
Add .... honey in a fine stream, beating constantly.
Add .... next 5 ingredients, mixing well.
Stir .... in oats and remaining ingredients.
Drop .... by spoonfuls onto greased cookie sheets.
Bake .... at 375 degrees for 10 minutes or until lightly browned.

Barb Cline
Bellingham, Washington

NATURAL CHOCOLATE CHIP COOKIES

1 c. butter, softened
2 eggs
3/4 c. molasses
1/2 c. honey
1 1/2 tsp. vanilla extract
1/3 c. wheat germ
1 1/4 c. whole wheat flour
3/4 tsp. each salt, soda
4 c. rolled oats
1 c. chunky peanut butter
1 12-oz. package chocolate chips

Combine .... first 5 ingredients in large bowl, mixing well.
Add .... remaining ingredients except chocolate chips, beating well.
Stir .... in chocolate chips.
Drop .... by teaspoonfuls onto greased baking sheets.
Bake .... at 325 degrees for 10 minutes or until lightly brown.
Yields ...... 6-7 dozen.

Candis Schey
Longmont, Colorado

HONEYED GRANOLA COOKIES

2 c. granola
3/4 c. whole wheat flour
1/4 tsp. salt
1/2 tsp. cinnamon
2 eggs, separated
2 tbsp. honey

Combine .... first 4 ingredients in bowl, mixing well.
Beat .... egg yolks, honey and 3/4 cup warm water together.
Add .... to granola mixture gradually, mixing well.
Fold .... stiffly beaten egg whites into batter.
Drop .... by spoonfuls onto greased cookie sheet.
Bake .... at 350 degrees for 30 minutes or until lightly browned.
Yields ...... 2 dozen cookies.

Mrs. Polly Webster
Lincoln, Maine

WHOLE WHEAT SUGAR COOKIES

1 tsp. baking powder
1/2 tsp. each salt, soda, nutmeg
1/2 c. butter, softened
2 tbsp. milk
1 tbsp. grated orange rind (opt.)
1 tsp. vanilla extract
1 egg
Sugar
2 c. whole wheat flour
1/2 tsp. cinnamon

Combine .... first 9 ingredients and 1 cup sugar together in large bowl, mixing well.
Stir .... flour into mixture.
Shape ...... into 1-inch balls.
Place .... 2 inches apart on cookie sheets, flattening slightly.
Combine .... 2 tablespoons sugar and cinnamon in bowl.
Sprinkle .... over cookies.
Bake .... at 375 degrees for 8 minutes or until lightly browned.

Carole Fisher
Martinsville, Indiana

CAROB CREPES

1 natural carob bar
1 1/2 c. flour
1/3 c. carob powder
1/2 tsp. baking powder
1/2 tsp. salt
2 c. milk
2 eggs
Melted butter
3/4 c. finely chopped dried apricots
6 tbsp. brown sugar
4 1/2 c. vanilla yogurt

Warm ...... carob bar at 200 degrees in oven.
Shave ...... with vegetable peeler to form carob curls, warming as often as necessary.
Combine .... next 4 ingredients in mixer bowl.
Beat .... in milk, eggs and 2 tablespoons butter until smooth.
Pour .... 2 tablespoons batter into hot greased 7-inch skillet; rotating pan to spread batter.
Turn .... to brown both sides.
Simmer ..... apricots and brown sugar with 3/4 cup water in saucepan until water is absorbed, stirring constantly.
Cool .... filling thoroughly.
Blend ...... in 3 cups yogurt.

Fill .... each crepe with 3 tablespoons apricot filling.
Roll .... and place seam side down on serving plate.
Garnish ..... with remaining yogurt and carob curls.
Yields ...... 24 crepes.

Photograph for this recipe on this page.

HONEY-VANILLA ICE MILK

4 c. milk
1/3 c. honey
1 1/2 tsp. vanilla extract
1/8 tsp. salt

Combine .... all ingredients in saucepan.
Heat .... until honey dissolves, stirring constantly.
Pour .... into ice cream freezer container.
Freeze ...... using manufacturer's directions.
Yields ...... 4-6 servings.

Ellen Hagan
Columbus, Georgia

VANILLA CUSTARD ICE CREAM

4 c. milk
4 eggs, separated
1/2 c. honey
1 tsp. arrowroot
2 tsp. vanilla extract

Scald .... milk in saucepan.
Beat .... egg yolks in bowl, adding honey in a fine stream.
Add .... arrowroot gradually.
Stir .... a small amount of hot milk into egg mixture; stir egg mixture into hot milk.
Simmer ..... until thickened, stirring constantly.
Chill .... for several hours.
Fold .... in vanilla extract and stiffly beaten egg whites.
Pour .... into ice cream freezer container.
Freeze ...... using manufacturer's directions.
Yields ...... 4-6 servings.

Carol Rees
Danville, Virginia

APRICOT-GRAPEFRUIT SHERBET

2/3 c. honey
1 1/4 c. grapefruit juice
1 c. apricot puree
1 tbsp. lemon juice
1 egg white, beaten stiff

Combine .... honey in saucepan with 1 cup water.
Boil .... for 5 minutes.
Combine .... syrup with next 3 ingredients in ice cream freezer container.
Freeze ...... using manufacturer's directions until slushy.
Fold .... in egg white.
Freeze ...... until of serving consistency.

Sue Bennett
Camden, New Jersey

LEMON-LIME BUTTERMILK SHERBET

4 c. buttermilk
1/4 c. honey
2 tbsp. lemon juice
2 tbsp. lime juice
1 tsp. finely grated lemon rind
1 tsp. finely grated lime rind

Place .... all ingredients in blender container.
Process ..... at medium speed until blended.
Pour .... into 9-inch square baking pan.
Freeze ...... covered, for 1 to 2 hours or until frozen around edges.
Place .... in bowl and beat until smooth.
Return ..... to square pan.
Freeze ...... until firm.
Thaw ...... for 10 minutes before serving.
Yields ...... 6-8 servings.

Dora Sterling
Comstock, Colorado

HONEY-RASPBERRY SHERBET

2 c. raspberries, mashed
2 tbsp. honey
1/2 c. orange juice
4 c. milk
2 egg whites, stiffly beaten

Combine .... first 4 ingredients in ice cream freezer container.

Freeze ...... using manufacturer's instructions until partially frozen.
Fold .... in egg whites.
Spoon ...... into freezer container.
Freeze ...... for several hours.
Yields ...... 4-6 servings.

Shirley May
Delon, Michigan

FROZEN STRAWBERRY YOGURT

1 10-oz. package frozen strawberries, thawed
2 tsp. gelatin
2 c. yogurt
3/4 c. sugar
1 tsp. vanilla extract
2 egg whites, stiffly beaten

Combine .... first 5 ingredients in large bowl, stirring well.
Fold .... egg whites gently into fruit mixture.
Freeze ...... in freezer container, using manufacturer's instructions.
Thaw ...... for 15 to 30 minutes before serving.
Garnish ..... with fresh fruit.
Yields ...... 6-8 servings.

Sharon L. Bouldin
Westerville, Ohio

APPLES IN WINE

2 lb. apples, peeled, sliced
1/4 c. butter
2 tbsp. honey
1/2 c. dry white wine
1/2 tsp. salt
1 tsp. grated lemon rind
1/4 tsp. nutmeg

Saute ...... apples in butter in skillet until golden brown.
Drizzle ..... honey over apples.
Add .... remaining ingredients and 1/2 cup water, mixing well.
Simmer ..... covered, for 20 minutes or until apples are tender-crisp.
Chill .... to serving temperature.

Jan Robards
Hollywood, Florida

APPLE-BREAD PUDDING WITH CUSTARD SAUCE

8 slices whole wheat bread, cubed, toasted
4 med. apples, chopped
1/8 tsp. salt
Fructose
1 tsp. cinnamon
1/2 c. golden raisins
9 eggs
4 1/4 c. milk
2 tsp. vanilla extract
4 tbsp. butter

Combine .... bread cubes, apples, salt, 1/2 cup fructose, cinnamon and raisins in large bowl.
Beat .... 3 eggs with 2 1/4 cups milk and 1 teaspoon vanilla in bowl until well mixed.
Pour .... over bread cube mixture.
Let .... stand for 15 minutes.
Pour .... into greased 2-quart baking dish.
Dot .... with butter.
Bake .... at 350 degrees for 1 hour or until center is firm.
Combine .... 6 eggs, 6 tablespoons fructose, 1 teaspoon vanilla and 2 cups milk in blender container.
Process ..... until smooth.
Pour .... into saucepan.
Simmer ..... for 5 minutes until thickened, stirring constantly.
Yields ...... 8-10 servings.

Photograph for this recipe on page 107.

BLUEBERRY CRUMBLE

1/4 c. butter
1/4 c. honey
1 egg
Dash of salt
1 tsp. soda
1/3 c. buttermilk or yogurt
1 1/3 c. whole wheat pastry flour
2 c. blueberries
1/4 c. butter
2 tbsp. honey
1/2 tsp. cinnamon

Combine .... first 6 ingredients and 1 cup flour in bowl, mixing well.
Spread ..... in greased baking dish.

Cover ...... with blueberries.
Mix .... remaining ingredients and 1/3 cup flour until crumbly.
Sprinkle .... over blueberries.
Bake .... at 350 degrees for 40 minutes or until lightly browned.
Yields ...... 6-8 servings.

Belinda Raymond
Reids, Virginia

GRAPEFRUIT MERINGUES

2 med. grapefruit, halved
2 egg whites
Dash of salt
2 tbsp. light brown sugar
3 tbsp. shredded coconut

Cut .... around each grapefruit section to loosen.
Beat .... egg whites until soft peaks form.
Add .... salt and sugar gradually, beating until stiff.
Fold .... in 2 tablespoons coconut.
Top .... grapefruit halves with meringue, sealing to edges.
Sprinkle .... with remaining coconut.
Bake .... at 325 degrees for 20 minutes or until brown.

Eloise Scott
Mooreville, Mississippi

GRAPES IN MINTED GINGER ALE

Green grapes
1 1/2 c. ginger ale
4 to 5 mint leaves or sprigs

Place .... 10 to 15 grapes in sherbet dish.
Add .... 1/4 to 1/2 cup ginger ale.
Garnish ..... with mint.
Yields ...... 4-5 servings.

Nancy Hickcox
South Burlington, Vermont

POACHED PEARS WITH SOFT CUSTARD

3/4 c. nonfat dry milk
4 eggs, beaten
1/4 tsp. salt
1 3/4 c. sugar
1 tbsp. butter

1/4 tsp. grated lemon rind
2 tsp. vanilla extract
8 pears, peeled

Combine . . . . dry milk with 2 cups water in saucepan, mixing well.

Stir . . . . in next 2 ingredients and 1/4 cup sugar.

Simmer . . . . . until mixture coats spoon, stirring constantly.

Stir . . . . in butter, lemon rind and 1 teaspoon vanilla.

Chill . . . . in refrigerator.

Add . . . . 1 1/2 cups sugar to 4 cups water in saucepan.

Simmer . . . . . for 5 minutes until sugar dissolves, stirring constantly.

Add . . . . 1 teaspoon vanilla and pears.

Simmer . . . . . for 1/2 hour or until pears are tender, turning occasionally.

Chill . . . . in syrup; drain.

Spoon . . . . . . custard into serving bowl.

Top . . . . with pears.

Yields . . . . . . 8 servings.

Photograph for this recipe on this page.

FANTASTIC STRAWBERRY FONDUE

2 tbsp. cornstarch
2 tbsp. sugar
2   10-oz. packages frozen strawberries, thawed, crushed
1   4-oz. carton whipped cream cheese, softened
1/4 c. Brandy (opt.)
Pound cake cubes
Marshmallows
Banana chunks
Angel food cake cubes

Blend . . . . . . cornstarch and sugar in a small amount of water in bowl.

Combine . . . . with strawberries in saucepan, blending well.

Cook . . . . until thick, stirring constantly.

Blend . . . . . . in cream cheese and Brandy, stirring until well mixed.

Pour . . . . into fondue pot over low heat.

Dip . . . . remaining ingredients into strawberry mixture with fondue forks.

Mary Carson
Selena, Ohio

ORANGE GRANOLA

2 c. oats
1 c. wheat germ
1/2 c. coconut
1/2 c. diced dates
2 tbsp. sesame seed
1/2 tsp. salt
1/2 c. sliced almonds
1/2 c. sunflower seed
1/3 c. oil
1/2 tsp. vanilla
1/2 c. packed brown sugar
1/4 c. frozen orange juice, thawed, undiluted
3/4 c. raisins

Combine . . . . first 8 ingredients in large bowl, mixing well.

Spread . . . . . onto baking pan.

Stir . . . . oil, vanilla and brown sugar into orange juice.

Pour . . . . over mixture.

Bake . . . . at 300 degrees until lightly browned, stirring occasionally.

Stir . . . . in raisins and cool to serving temperature.

Frannie York
Oak Park, Illinois

TOASTY NUT GRANOLA

6 c. oats
1/2 c. packed brown sugar
3/4 c. wheat germ
1/2 c. freshly grated coconut
1/4 c. sesame seed
1 c. chopped pecans
1/2 c. oil
1/4 c. honey
1/2 tsp. vanilla extract

Spread . . . . . oats in 2 shallow baking pans.
Bake . . . . at 350 degrees for 10 minutes.
Combine . . . . with remaining ingredients in bowl, mixing well.
Spoon . . . . . . into 2 baking pans.
Bake . . . . at 350 degrees for 10 minutes or until brown, stirring occasionally; cool.
Store . . . . in airtight container.

Diann Ferris
Waterloo, Indiana

Learn to eat more slowly.

HONEY MERINGUES

1/3 c. honey
3 egg whites
Pinch of salt
1/4 tsp. cream of tartar
1 to 2 tsp. vanilla extract

Combine . . . . honey with 1/3 cup water in saucepan.
Cook . . . . for about 10 minutes or to soft-ball stage.
Beat . . . . egg whites in bowl until soft peaks form.
Add . . . . salt and cream of tartar gradually, beating until stiff.
Drizzle . . . . . syrup into egg whites, beating for about 5 minutes or until cool.
Beat . . . . in vanilla.
Drop . . . . by spoonfuls on parchment paper-lined baking sheet.
Bake . . . . . . at 350 degrees for 18 minutes or until lightly browned.
Cool . . . . on wire rack.
Fill . . . . with custard or fruit filling.
Yields . . . . . . 4-6 servings.

Jane Seymore
Henry, Colorado

SLIMMER'S STRAWBERRY PIE

1 env. low-calorie strawberry gelatin
1 20-oz. box frozen strawberries
1 graham cracker pie shell
1 c. low-calorie whipped topping

Dissolve . . . . gelatin in 1 cup boiling water.
Stir . . . . in strawberries until thawed.
Spoon . . . . . . into pie shell.
Chill . . . . until firm.
Swirl . . . . whipped topping over top before serving.

Rose Mayer
Fargo, North Dakota

PUMPKIN PIE

1 14-oz. can pumpkin
2 packets Sweet 'N Low
1/2 tsp. salt
1 1/4 c. skim milk
1 tsp. ginger
1/2 tsp. each nutmeg, cinnamon
2 eggs, well beaten

Combine . . . . all ingredients in bowl, mixing well.
Pour . . . . into 9-inch pie plate.
Bake . . . . at 375 degrees for 1 hour or until knife inserted in center comes out clean.

Ila Preston
Kalamazoo, Michigan

LEMON LITE PIE

2 pkg. low-calorie lemon gelatin
2 pkg. whipped topping mix, prepared
1 9-in. graham cracker pie shell

Prepare . . . . . gelatin according to package directions using half the water.
Stir . . . . in 10 ice cubes until gelatin thickens.
Fold . . . . in whipped topping.
Pour . . . . into pie shell.
Chill . . . . until serving time.

Lily Bracken
Portland, Oregon

LUSH LIME PIE

1 qt. ice milk
1 6-oz. can frozen limeade concentrate

Green food coloring (opt.)
1 8-in. graham cracker pie shell

Beat .... ice milk in bowl until soft.
Add .... limeade concentrate gradually, beating until smooth.
Stir .... in food coloring and pour into pie shell.
Freeze ...... until firm.
Garnish ..... with lime slices.

Alice Carrington
Wildcat Shoals, Arkansas

SUGARLESS APPLE PIE

1 6-oz. can frozen apple juice concentrate
2 tbsp. cornstarch
1 tbsp. margarine
1 tsp. cinnamon
Salt to taste
5 lg. apples, peeled, sliced
1 recipe 2-crust pie pastry
Melted margarine

Heat .... apple juice with cornstarch in saucepan, stirring constantly.
Stir .... in next 3 ingredients.
Pour .... over apples in bowl, mixing carefully.
Spoon ...... into pastry-lined pie plate; cover with remaining pastry.
Brush ...... crust with margarine.
Bake .... in moderate oven until golden brown.

Darlene Ehman
Portland, Oregon

WHOLE WHEAT PIE CRUST

1 1/4 c. whole wheat pastry flour
3 tbsp. butter
3 tbsp. oil

Combine .... flour, butter and oil in bowl.
Cut .... with pastry blender until crumbly.
Stir .... in 2 tablespoons ice water, stirring until mixture forms ball.
Roll .... on floured surface to fit 9-inch pie plate.
Place .... in pie plate and flute edge.
Bake .... at 425 degrees for 12 minutes or until lightly browned.

Ann Graves
Scranton, Pennsylvania

COCONUT-OAT PIE CRUST

3/4 c. rolled oats
3/4 c. whole wheat pastry flour
1/4 c. coconut
1/3 c. oil

Place .... oats in blender container.
Process ..... to consistency of coarse flour.
Combine .... with remaining ingredients and 2 tablespoons ice water in bowl, mixing well.
Press .... to about 1/8-inch thickness in greased 9-inch pie plate.
Bake .... at 425 degrees for 12 minutes or until lightly browned.

Wanda Sikes
Rock Springs, Virginia

SLIM CREAM PUFFS

1 tbsp. oil
1/4 c. sifted flour
Salt to taste
1 egg
3/4 c. skim milk
3/4 tsp. cornstarch
2 tbsp. sugar
1 egg yolk, beaten
1/4 tsp. vanilla extract
Confectioners' sugar

Combine .... first 3 ingredients with 1/4 cup water in saucepan, mixing well.
Heat .... to boiling point, stirring constantly.
Beat .... in egg until well mixed.
Drop .... by teaspoonfuls onto cookie sheet.
Bake .... at 375 degrees for 40 minutes or until lightly browned.
Cool .... and slit.
Combine .... milk, cornstarch and sugar in saucepan, mixing well.
Heat .... to boiling point, stirring constantly.
Stir .... a small amount of hot mixture into egg yolk; stir egg yolk into hot mixture.
Simmer ..... until thick, stirring constantly.
Stir .... in vanilla; cool.
Spoon ...... into cream puffs.
Dust .... with confectioners' sugar.

Corinne McGuiggan
Revere, Massachusetts

calories do count

Almonds, shelled, 1/4 cup 213
Apples: 1 med 70
   chopped, 1/2 cup 30
Apple juice, 1 cup 117
Applesauce: sweetened, 1/2 cup 115
   unsweetened, 1/2 cup 50
Apricots: fresh, 3 55
   canned, 1/2 cup 110
   dried, 10 halves 100
Apricot nectar, 1 cup 140
Asparagus: fresh, 6 spears 19
   canned, 1/2 cup 18
Avocado, 1 med. 265
Bacon, 2 sl. crisp-cooked, drained 90
Banana, 1 med. 100
Beans: baked, 1/2 cup 160
   dry, 1/2 cup 350
   green, 1/2 cup 20
   lima, 1/2 cup 95
   soy, 1/2 cup 95
Bean sprouts, 1/2 cup 18
Beef, cooked, 3 oz. serving:
   roast, rib 375
   roast, heel of round 165
   steak, sirloin 330
Beer, 12 oz. 150
Beets, cooked, 1/2 cup 40
Biscuit, from mix, 1 90
Bologna, all meat, 3 oz. 235
Bread: roll, 1 85
   white, 1 slice 65
   whole wheat, 1 slice 65
Bread crumbs, dry, 1 cup 390
Broccoli, cooked, 1/2 cup 20
Butter: 1/2 cup 800
   1 tbsp. 100
Buttermilk, 1 cup 90
Cabbage: cooked, 1/2 cup 15
   fresh, shredded, 1/2 cup 10
Cake: angel food, 1/12 pkg. prepared ..140
   devil's food, 1/12 pkg. prepared 195
   yellow, 1/12 pkg. prepared 200
Candy: caramel, 1 oz. 115
   chocolate, sweet, 1 oz. 145
   hard candy, 1 oz. 110
   marshmallows, 1 oz. 90
Cantaloupe, 1/2 med. 60
Carrots, cooked, 1/2 cup 23
   fresh, 1 med. 20
Catsup, 1 tbsp. 18
Cauliflower: cooked, 1/2 cup 13
   fresh, 1/2 lb. 60
Celery, chopped, 1/2 cup 8

Cereals: bran flakes, 1/2 cup 53
   corn flakes, 1/2 cup 50
   oatmeal, cooked, 1/2 cup 65
Cheese: American, 1 oz. 105
   Cheddar: 1 oz. 113
     shredded, 1 cup 452
   cottage: creamed, 1/2 cup 130
     uncreamed, 1/2 cup 85
   cream: 1 oz. 107
   mozzarella, 1 oz. 80
     shredded, 1 cup 320
   Parmesan, 1 oz. 110
   Velveeta, 1 oz. 84
Cherries: canned, sour in water, 1/2 cup 53
   fresh, sweet, 1/2 cup 40
Chicken, meat only, 4 oz. serving:
   boned, chopped, 1/2 cup 170
   broiled 155
   canned, boned 230
   roast, dark meat 210
   roast, light meat 207
Chili peppers: green, fresh, 1/2 lb. .. 62
   red, fresh, 1/2 lb. 108
Chili powder with seasoning, 1 tbsp. .. 51
Chocolate, baking, 1 oz. 143
Cocoa mix, 1-oz. package 115
Cocoa powder, baking, 1/3 cup 120
Coconut, dried, shredded, 1/4 cup 166
Coffee 0
Corn: canned, cream-style, 1/2 cup 100
   canned, whole kernel, 1/2 cup 85
Corn bread, mix, prepared, 1 x 4-in. piece 125
Corn chips, 1 oz. 130
Cornmeal, 1/2 cup 264
Cornstarch, 1 tbsp. 29
Crab, fresh, meat only, 3 oz. 80
   canned, 3 oz. 85
Crackers: graham, 2 1/2-in. square 28
   Ritz, each 17
   saltine, 2-in. square 13
Cracker crumbs, 1/2 cup 281
Cranberries: fresh, 1/2 lb. 100
   juice, cocktail, 1 cup 163
   sauce, 1/2 cup 190
Cream: half-and-half, 1 tbsp. 20
   heavy, 1 tbsp 55
   light, 1 tbsp. 30
Creamer, imitation powdered, 1 tsp. ... 10
Cucumber, 1 med. 30
Dates, dried, chopped, 1/2 cup 244
Eggs: 1 whole, large 80
   1 white 17
   1 yolk 59

Eggplant, cooked, 1/2 cup 19
Fish sticks, 5 200
Flour: rye, 1 cup 286
  white: 1 cup 420
  1 tbsp. 28
  whole wheat, 1 cup 400
Fruit cocktail, canned, 1/2 cup 98
Garlic, 1 clove 2
Gelatin, unflavored, 1 env. 25
Grapes: fresh, 1/2 cup 35-50
  juice, 1 cup 170
Grapefruit: fresh, 1/2 med. 60
  juice, unsweetened, 1 cup 100
Ground beef, patty, lean 185
  regular 245
Haddock, fried, 3 oz. .140
Ham, 3 oz. servings:
  boiled 200
  fresh, roast 320
  country-style 335
  cured, lean 160
Honey, 1 tbsp. 65
Ice cream, 1/2 cup 135
Ice milk, 1/2 cup 96
Jams and preserves, 1 tbsp. 54
Jellies, 1 tbsp. 55
Jell-O, 1/2 cup 80
Lamb, 3 oz. serving, leg roast 185
  1 1/2 oz., rib chop .175
Lemon juice, 1 tbsp. 4
Lemonade, sweetened, 1 cup 110
Lentils, cooked, 1/2 cup 168
Lettuce, 1 head 40
Liver, 2 oz. serving: beef, fried 130
  chicken, simmered 88
Lobster, 2 oz. 55
Macaroni, cooked, 1/2 cup 90
Mango, 1 fresh 134
Margarine: 1/2 cup 800
  1 tbsp. 100
Mayonnaise: 1 tbsp. 100
Milk: whole, 1 cup 160
  skim, 1 cup 89
  condensed, 1 cup 982
  evaporated, 1 cup 345
  dry nonfat, 1 cup 251
Muffin, plain 120
Mushrooms: canned, 1/2 cup 20
  fresh, 1 lb. 123
Mustard: prepared, brown, 1 tbsp. 13
  prepared, yellow, 1 tbsp. 10
Nectarine, 1 fresh 30
Noodles: egg, cooked, 1/2 cup 100
  fried, chow mein, 2 oz. 275
Oil, cooking, salad, 1 tbsp. 120
Okra, cooked, 8 pods 25
Olives: green, 3 lg. 15
  ripe, 2 lg. 15

Onion: chopped, 1/2 cup 32
  dehydrated flakes, 1 tbsp. 17
  green, 6 20
  whole, 1 40
Orange: 1 whole 65
  juice, 1 cup 115
Oysters, meat only, 1/2 cup 80
Pancakes, 4-in. diameter, 1 60
Peaches: fresh, 1 med. 35
  canned, 1/2 cup 100
  dried, 1/2 cup 210
Peanuts, shelled, roasted, 1 cup 420
Peanut butter, 1 tbsp. 100
Pears: fresh, 1 med. 100
  canned, 1/2 cup 97
  dried, 1/2 cup 214
Peas: black-eyed, 1/2 cup 70
  green, canned, 1/2 cup 83
  green, frozen, 1/2 cup 69
Pecans, chopped, 1/2 cup 400
Peppers: sweet green, 1 med. 14
  sweet red, 1 med. 19
Perch, white, 4 oz. 50
Pickles: dill, 1 lg. 15
  sweet, 1 average 30
Pie crust, mix, 1 crust 626
Pie, 8-in. frozen, 1/6 serving
  apple 234
  cherry 300
  peach 280
Pimento, canned, 1 avg. 10
Pineapple: fresh, diced, 1/2 cup 36
  canned, 1/2 cup 90
  juice, 1 cup 135
Plums: fresh, 1 med. 30
  canned, 3 101
Popcorn, plain, popped, 1 cup 54
Pork, cooked, lean:
  Boston butt, roasted, 4 oz. 280
  chop, broiled, 3.5 oz. 260
  loin, roasted, 4 oz. .290
Potato chips, 1 oz. 322
Potatoes, white:
  baked, 1 sm. with skin 93
  boiled, 1 sm. 70
  French-fried, 10 pieces 155
  hashed brown, 1/2 cup 225
  mashed, with milk and butter, 1/2 cup 90
Potatoes, sweet:
  baked, 1 avg. 155
  candied, 1 avg. 295
  canned, 1/2 cup 110
Prune: 1 lg. 19
  dried, cooked, 1/2 cup 137
  juice, 1 cup 197
Puddings and pie fillings, prepared:
  banana, 1/2 cup 165
  butterscotch, 1/2 cup 190

chocolate, 1/2 cup 190
lemon, 1/2 cup 125
Puddings, instant, prepared:
banana, 1/2 cup 175
butterscotch, 1/2 cup 175
chocolate, 1/2 cup 200
lemon, 1/2 cup 180
Pumpkin, canned, 1/2 cup 38
Raisins, dried, 1/2 cup 231
Rice: cooked, white, 1/2 cup 90
cooked, brown, 1/2 cup 100
precooked, 1/2 cup .105
Salad dressings, commercial:
blue cheese, 1 tbsp. 75
French, 1 tbsp. 70
Italian, 1 tbsp. 83
mayonnaise, 1 tbsp. .100
mayonnaise-type, 1 tbsp. 65
Russian, 1 tbsp. 75
Thousand Island, 1 tbsp. 80
Salami, cooked, 2 oz. .180
Salmon: canned, 4 oz. 180
steak, 4 oz. 220
Sardines, canned, 3 oz. 175
Sauces: barbecue, 1 tbsp. 17
hot pepper, 1 tbsp. 3
soy, 1 tbsp. 9
white, med., 1/2 cup 215
Worcestershire, 1 tbsp. 15
Sauerkraut, 1/2 cup 21
Sausage, cooked, 2 oz. 260
Sherbet, 1/2 cup 130
Shrimp: cooked, 3 oz. 50
canned, 4 oz. 130
Soft drinks, 1 cup 100
Soup, 1 can, condensed:
chicken with rice 116
cream of celery 215
cream of chicken 235
cream of mushroom 331
tomato 220
vegetable-beef 198
Sour cream, 1/2 cup .240
Spaghetti, cooked, 1/2 cup 80
Spinach: fresh, 1/2 lb. 60

cooked, 1/2 cup 20
Squash: summer, cooked, 1/2 cup 15
winter, cooked, 1/2 cup 65
Strawberries, fresh, 1/2 cup 23
Sugar: brown, packed, 1/2 cup 410
confectioners', sifted, 1/2 cup 240
granulated: 1/2 cup 385
1 tbsp. 48
Syrups: chocolate, 1 tbsp. 50
corn, 1 tbsp. 58
maple, 1 tbsp. 50
Taco shell, 1 shell 50
Tea, 1 cup 0
Tomatoes: fresh, 1 med. 40
canned, 1/2 cup 25
juice, 1 cup 45
paste, 6 oz. can 150
sauce, 8-oz. can 34
Toppings: caramel, 1 tbsp. 70
chocolate fudge, 1 tbsp. 65
Cool Whip, 1 tbsp. 14
Dream Whip, prepared, 1 tbsp. 8
strawberry, 1 tbsp. 60
Tortilla, corn, 1 65
Tuna: canned in oil, drained, 4 oz. 230
canned in water, 4 oz. 144
Turkey: dark meat, roasted, 4 oz. 230
light meat, roasted, 4 oz. 200
Veal: cutlet, broiled, 3 oz. 185
roast, 3 oz. 230
Vegetable juice cocktail, 1 cup 43
Vinegar, 1 tbsp. 2
Waffles, 1 130
Walnuts, chopped, 1/2 cup 410
Water chestnuts, sliced, 1/2 cup 25
Watermelon, fresh, cubed, 1/2 cup 26
Wheat germ, 1 tbsp. 29
Wine: dessert, 1/2 cup 140
table, 1/2 cup 85
Yeast: compressed, 1 oz. 24
dry, 1 oz. 80
Yogurt: plain, w/whole milk, 1 cup 153
plain, w/skim milk, 1 cup 123
with fruit, 1 cup 260

nutrition labeling

Modern Americans have become very diet and nutrition conscious, and in response, commercial food producers have begun to include nutrition information on the labels of their products. Nutrition Labeling is an invaluable service in many ways. There are many persons on special diets (diabetic, low-sodium, low-cholesterol) who must know the specifics of the foods they eat. However, whether the homemaker cooks for a special diet or not, Nutrition Labeling on the foods she buys helps her to know the part they play in her overall nutrition and menu planning.

The United States Food and Drug Administration has determined how much of every important nutrient is needed by the average healthy person in the United States, well known as the Recommended Daily Dietary Allowance (RDA). The United States RDA reflects the highest amounts of nutritives for all ages and sexes. Pregnant and nursing women, as well as persons with special dietary needs, should consult their doctors for any recommended increases or decreases in their daily diet.

UNITED STATES RECOMMENDED DAILY ALLOWANCE CHART

Protein	45-65 Grams
Carbohydrates	125 Grams
Vitamin A	5,000 International Units
Thiamine (Vitamin B_1)	1.5 Milligrams
Riboflavin (Vitamin B_2)	1.7 Milligrams
Vitamin B_6	2 Milligrams
Vitamin B_{12}	6 Micrograms
Folic Acid (B Vitamin)	0.4 Milligrams
Pantothenic Acid (B Vitamin)	10 Milligrams
Vitamin C (Ascorbic Acid)	55-60 Milligrams
Vitamin D	400 International Units
Vitamin E	30 International Units
Iron	18 Milligrams
Calcium	1 Gram
Niacin (Nicotinic Acid)	13-20 Milligrams
Magnesium	400 Milligrams
Zinc	15 Milligrams
Copper	2 Milligrams
Phosphorus	1 Gram
Iodine	150 Micrograms
Biotin (Vitamin H)	0.3 Milligrams

IMPORTANT NUTRIENTS YOUR DIET REQUIRES

PROTEIN

Why? Absolutely essential in building, repairing and renewing of all body tissue. Helps body resist infection. Builds enzymes and hormones, helps form and maintain body fluids.

Where? Milk, eggs, lean meats, poultry, fish, soybeans, peanuts, dried peas and beans, grains and cereals.

CARBOHYDRATES

Why?   Provide needed energy for bodily functions, provide warmth, as well as fuel for brain and nerve tissues. Lack of carbohydrates will cause body to use protein for energy rather than for repair and building.

Where?   Sugars: sugar, table syrups, jellies and jams, etc., as well as dried and fresh fruits. Starches: cereals, pasta, rice, corn, dried beans and peas, potatoes, stem and leafy vegetables, and milk.

FATS

Why?   Essential in the use of fat soluble vitamins (A, D, E, K), and fatty acids. Have more than twice the concentrated energy than equal amount of carbohydrate for body energy and warmth.

Where?   Margarine, butter, cooking oil, mayonnaise, vegetable shortening, milk, cream, ice cream, cheese, meat, fish, eggs, poultry, chocolate, coconut, nuts.

VITAMIN A

Why?   Needed for healthy skin and hair, as well as for healthy, infection-resistant mucous membranes.

Where?   Dark green, leafy and yellow vegetables, liver. Deep yellow fruits, such as apricots and cantaloupe. Milk, cheese, eggs, as well as fortified margarine and butter.

THIAMINE (VITAMIN B_1)

Why?   Aids in the release of energy of foods, as well as in normal appetite and digestion. Promotes healthy nervous system.

Where?   Pork, liver, kidney. Dried peas and beans. Whole grain and enriched breads and cereals.

RIBOFLAVIN (VITAMIN B_2)

Why?   Helps to oxidize foods. Promotes healthy eyes and skin, especially around mouth and eyes. Prevents pellagra.

Where?   Meat, especially liver and kidney, as well as milk, cheese, eggs. Dark leafy vegetables. Enriched bread and cereal products. Almonds, dried peas and beans.

VITAMIN B_6

Why?   Helps protein in building body tissues. Needed for healthy nerves, skin and digestion. Also helps body to use fats and carbohydrates for energy.

Where?   Milk, wheat germ, whole grain and fortified cereals. Liver and kidney, pork and beef.

VITAMIN B_{12}

Why?   Aids body in formation of red blood cells, as well as in regular work of all body cells.

Where?   Lean meats, milk, eggs, fish, cheese, as well as liver and kidney.

FOLIC ACID

Why?   Aids in healthy blood system, as well as intestinal tract. Helps to prevent anemia.

Where?   Green leaves of vegetables and herbs, as well as liver and milk. Wheat germ and soybeans.

PANTOTHENIC ACID

Why?   Aids in proper function of digestive system.

Where?   Liver, kidney and eggs. Peanuts and molasses. Broccoli and other vegetables.

VITAMIN C (ASCORBIC ACID)

Why?   Promotes proper bone and tooth formation. Helps body utilize iron and resist infection. Strengthens blood vessels. Lack of it causes bones to heal slowly, failure of wounds to heal and fragile vessels to bleed easily.

Where?   Citrus fruits, cantaloupe and strawberries. Broccoli, kale, green peppers, raw cabbage, sweet potatoes, cauliflower, tomatoes.

VITAMIN D
Why?   Builds strong bones and teeth by aiding utilization of calcium and phosphorus.
Where?   Fortified milk, fish liver oils, as well as salmon, tuna and sardines. Also eggs.

VITAMIN E
Why?   Needed in maintaining red blood cells.
Where?   Whole grain cereals, wheat germ, and beans and peas, lettuce and eggs.

IRON
Why?   Used with protein for hemoglobin production. Forms nucleus of each cell, and helps them to use oxygen.
Where?   Kidney and liver, as well as shellfish, lean meats, and eggs. Deep yellow and dark green leafy vegetables. Dried peas, beans, fruits. Potatoes, whole grain cereals and bread. Enriched flour and bread. Dark molasses.

CALCIUM
Why?   Builds and renews bones, teeth, other tissues, as well as aiding in the proper function of muscles, nerves and heart. Controls normal blood clotting. With protein, aids in oxidation of foods.
Where?   Milk and milk products, excluding butter. Dark green vegetables, oysters, clams and sardines.

NIACIN
Why?   Helps body to oxidize food. Aids in digestion, and helps to keep nervous system and skin healthy.
Where?   Peanuts, liver, tuna, as well as fish, poultry and lean meats. Enriched breads, cereals and peas.

MAGNESIUM
Why?   Aids nervous system and sleep.
Where?   Almonds, peanuts, raisins and prunes. Vegetables, fruits, milk, fish and meats.

ZINC
Why?   Needed for cell formation.
Where?   Nuts and leafy green vegetables. Shellfish.

COPPER
Why?   Helps body to utilize iron.
Where?   Vegetables and meats.

PHOSPHORUS
Why?   Maintains normal blood clotting function, as well as builds bones, teeth and nerve tissue. Aids in utilization of sugar and fats.
Where?   Oatmeal and whole wheat products. Eggs and cheese, dried beans and peas. Nuts, lean meats, and fish and poultry.

IODINE
Why?   Enables thyroid gland to maintain proper body metabolism.
Where?   Iodized salt. Saltwater fish and seafood. Milk and vegetables.

BIOTIN (VITAMIN H)
Why?   Helps to maintain body cells.
Where?   Eggs and liver. Any foods rich in Vitamin B.

index

PHOTOGRAPHY CREDITS

Cover: United Fresh Fruit and Vegetable Association; Ruth Lundgren, Ltd.; Olive Administrative Committee; Washington State Apple Commission; California Raisin Advisory Board; National Turkey Federation; American Lamb Council; American Dry Milk Institute, Inc.; National Live Stock and Meat Board; American Dairy Association; The McIlhenny Company (Tabasco); Tuna Research Foundation; California Apricot Advisory Board; The J. M. Smucker Co.; Spanish Green Olive Commission; The American Mushroom Institute; National Macaroni Institute; National Dairy Council; Standard Brands: Fleischmann's Margarine, Fleischmann's Yeast; Kellogg Company; Welch Foods Inc.; Fructose; Carnation Company — Instant Product Division; Pet, Inc.; and El Molino — Cara Coa Brand.

COOK LITE & EAT RIGHT

The Be-Good-To-Yourself Cookbook

FOR ORDERING INFORMATION

Write To:

FAVORITE RECIPES PRESS
P. O. Box 77
Nashville, Tennessee 37202

Or Call:

Toll Free Cookbook Hotline

1-800-251-1520

Tennesseans Call

1-800-342-4067

Library of Congress Cataloging in Publication Data
Main entry under title:
Cook lite & eat right.
   (Favorite recipes of home economics teachers)
   Includes index.
   1. Cookery.   I. Favorite Recipes Press.   II. Title:
Cook lite and eat right.   III. Series.
TX715.C7637   1983   641.5'63   83-8926
ISBN 0-87197-151-8